SCIENCE FAIR PROJECTS

Flight, Space & Astronomy

Bob Bonnet & Dan Keen
Illustrated by Frances Zweifel

Sterling Publishing Co., Inc.
New York

Edited by Claire Bazinet

Library of Congress Cataloging-in-Publication Data
Bonnet, Robert L.
    Science fair projects: flight, space & astronomy / Bob Bonnet and Dan Keen;
illustrated by Frances Zweifel.
    p.   cm.
    Includes index.
    Summary: Presents fifty-three simple experiments and projects revolving around
space science, including topics such as seasons, the night sky, light, and flight.
    ISBN 0-8069-9450-9
    1. Space sciences—Experiments—Juvenile literature. 2. Astronautics—Experiments—
Juvenile literature. 3. Astronomy—Experiments—Juvenile literature. 4. Science—Exhibitions—
Juvenile literature. 5. Science projects—Juvenile literature. [1. Space sciences—Experiments.
2. Experiments. 3. Science projects.] I. Keen, Dan. II. Zweifel, Frances, ill. III. Title.
QB500.22.B66   1997   96-39281
520'.78—dc21   CIP
                                                                              AC

10 9 8 7 6 5 4 3 2

First paperback edition published in 1998 by
Sterling Publishing Company, Inc.
387 Park Avenue South, New York, N.Y. 10016
© 1997 by Bob Bonnet and Dan Keen
Distributed in Canada by Sterling Publishing
% Canadian Manda Group, One Atlantic Avenue, Suite 105
Toronto, Ontario, Canada M6K 3E7
Distributed in Great Britain and Europe by Cassell PLC
Wellington House, 125 Strand, London WC2R 0BB, England
Distributed in Australia by Capricorn Link (Australia) Pty Ltd.
P.O. Box 6651, Baulkham Hills, Business Centre, NSW 2153, Australia
Manufactured in the United States of America

Sterling ISBN 0-8069-9450-9 Trade
            0-8069-9482-7 Paper

CONTENTS

A Note to the Parent

People have always looked up at the sky and the things in it with awe and wonder. That fascination creates an exciting desire to learn about our universe. The world we see above and around us is a unique part of our environment.

This book provides a selection of science projects about flight, astronomy and space. It offers a blend of many science disciplines: math, physics, aerodynamics, optics and astronomy. The concepts presented include: devices that move through the air, air pressure, lighter-than-air objects, lunar calendars and phases, constellations, solar effects, and much more. Your young people will work with kites, parachutes, balloons, bubbles, compasses, binoculars and telescopes to learn about science.

Science should be enjoyable, interesting and thought-provoking—that is the concept the writers wish to convey. While this book presents many scientific ideas and learning techniques that are valuable and useful, the approach is designed to entice the child with the excitement and fun of scientific investigation.

The material is presented in a light and interesting fashion. For example, the concept of measurement can be demonstrated by teaching precise measuring in inches or centimeters, or by having a child stretch his or her arms around a tree trunk and asking, "Are all children's reaches the same?" We present science in a way that does not seem like science.

The scientific concepts introduced here will form a basis to help the young student later understand more advanced scientific principles. Projects will develop those science skills needed in our ever increasingly complex society: skills such as classifying objects, making measured observations, thinking clearly and accurately recording data. Values are dealt with in a general way. One should never harm any living thing just for the sake of it. Respect for life should be fundamental. Disruption of natural processes should not occur thoughtlessly and unnecessarily. Interference with ecological systems should always be avoided.

The activities presented in this book target third- through fifth-grade students. The materials needed to do most of the activities are commonly found around the home or easily available at minimal cost.

Because safety is and must always be the first consideration, we recommend that all activities be done under adult supervision. Even seemingly harmless objects can become a hazard under certain circumstances. For example, a bowling ball can be a danger, if it is allowed to fall on a child's foot.

There are many benefits in store for a child who chooses to do a science project. It motivates the child to learn. Doing such an activity helps develop thinking skills; it prompts a child to question and learn how to solve problems. In these activities, the child is asked to make observations using all the senses and to record those observations accurately and honestly. Quantitative measurements of distance, size and volume must be made. Students may find a subject so interesting that, after the project is completed, they will want to do more investigation on their own. Spin-off interests can develop, too. In doing a science project about weather, while using a computer to record weather data, a child may discover an interest in computers.

The authors recommend that parents take an active interest in their child's science project. Apart from the safety aspect, when a parent is involved, contact time between the parent and child increases. Such quality time strengthens relationships, as well as the child's self-esteem. Working on a project is an experience that can be shared. An involved parent is telling the child that he or she believes education is important. Parents should support the academic learning process at least as much as they support Little League, music lessons, or any other growth activity. Parents should help the student in reading, understanding and completing these educational and fun projects.

Adults can be an invaluable resource for information that the child draws upon, sharing acquired knowledge and their own life experiences. By providing transportation, taking the child to a library or other places for research, they can also stretch the child's world. In our school, one student doing a project on insects was taken by his parents to the Mosquito Commission Laboratory, where he talked with professionals in the field.

Many projects in this book have been designed as "around-you science," in contrast to "book science." By "around-you science" we mean doing a science project right where you are—in your home, your neighborhood, your school. Getting ideas for a science fair project can even begin right at your feet. What is living under that old board lying on the ground? What species of insects are lying on your windowsill, trapped by the screen? Are termites eating your house? How many rings can you count in the trunk of the tree your neighbor has just cut down? Are some rings closer together than others? How many stars can you see with your naked eye on a clear night? Get excited with your child about the world around us!

Clear and creative thought is a primary goal for the young scientific mind. This book will help prepare a young person for future involvement and satisfying experiences in the field of science.

Bob Bonnet and Dan Keen

Project 1
Who's in the Moon?
Imagination and moon images

Have you ever heard anyone talk about the Man in the Moon? Some people say that, when they look up at the moon, they see a face looking down. Long ago, some ancient peoples feared the power of the moon, while others worshiped it and were happy that the moon kept watch at night.

You need
- clear evening with a full moon
- pencil and paper
- clipboard (optional)

When you look up at the moon from Earth, the light and dark patterns you see there can form shapes. Today we know, because we have been there and seen the moon's surface close up, that those light and dark patterns are the mountains, giant craters and waterless seas on the moon. We have even mapped the moon's surface in great detail.

On an evening when the moon is full, take a pad or a clipboard with paper and draw the shapes you see. Then use your imagination. Can you see a face in the shapes you have drawn? If so, is it the face of a man or woman, or do you see a boy, a girl or some sort of animal?

Just as the ancient people used their imaginations to see creatures in the patterns of the stars, use your imagination to fill in details of your "Face in the Moon," adding ears, hair, a body shape and anything else you see. Give the figure a name and write a story telling who it is and how it came to be in the moon.

Project 2

"Three, Two, One..."

A matter of action and reaction

"For every action there is an equal and opposite reaction." This law of physics was first discovered by Sir Isaac Newton in 1687. Suppose you and your friend are both wearing roller skates and your friend is standing in front of you. If you push him, he will roll away in the direction of your push, but you will roll, too. A force that is equal but opposite acts to push you backwards!

You need
- use of a flagpole
- a long, oblong balloon
- 2 small paper clips
- adhesive tape
- string
- a friend

Gases or liquids are sometimes pushed through an opening to move, or propel, an object forward. This principle is called "jet propulsion." This is how jet airplanes, missiles and rockets move through the air and even maneuver in outer space.

Tie a piece of string or fishing line to the rope on a flagpole used to raise a flag. Pull on the rope so that the string is pulled to the top of the flagpole. Have a friend hold the other end of the string.

Blow up an oblong-shaped balloon. Pinch the neck to keep the air inside the balloon.

Have your friend bend one end of a paper clip to form an "L" shape. Bend a second paper clip the same way.

Using sticky tape, fasten the L-shape leg of both paper clips onto the same side of the balloon, one near the neck end that you are holding and the other near the closed end. Hook both paper clips onto the string on the flagpole so that the balloon's neck is towards you.

The string should be pulled tight by your friend and kept straight. Let go of the balloon's neck. Rushing to escape, the air inside the balloon will push against the inside front wall and the balloon will shoot straight up along the string like a rocket.

How high do you think it will go? Is the force of gravity stronger than the force of the escaping air that pushes the balloon forward, or will the balloon continue to shoot upward until it runs out of air?

What kind of path would the balloon take if you didn't have it on a string to keep it going in a straight line? If you used a shorter rod, say about three feet (90 cm) in length, instead of a long string, would the balloon continue on in a straight line after it left the end of the rod?

Project 3
Going Up?
Hot air rising

Hot air rises, which is partially the cause of tornadoes and other weather conditions.

You need
- glycerin
- water
- pipe cleaner
- use of a toaster
- small bowl
- liquid soap
- kitchen measuring cup
- tablespoon
- an adult

In June of 1783, in France, a large bag made of paper was filled with hot air and smoke from a fire. The bag floated up to about 6,000 feet. It was the beginning of hot-air balloons, used today to carry weather instruments high above the Earth, and the popular sport of hot-air ballooning. Your challenge: prove that hot air rises.

You will need some bubble solution, either bought or homemade. To make your own bubble solution, pour ½ measuring cup of water into a bowl. Add ¼ cup of liquid soap, such as dishwashing detergent or liquid hand soap. Have an adult measure out and add one tablespoon of glycerin. (Glycerin should be handled carefully, and by an adult. You must not get any in your mouth, or place the glycerin near anything hot—because it can catch fire.) Use the tablespoon to stir your solution.

If a bubble wand didn't come with the bought solution, make one by bending one end of a pipe cleaner into a circle about the size of a large coin or bottle cap.

On a table or countertop, have an adult plug in a toaster and push down the handle, as if to toast a slice of bread. Be very careful, because toasters get very hot. Keep the bubble solution—in fact, any liquids—away from the toaster.

Dip the wand into your bubble solution. Stand about two to three feet (60-90 cm) away from the toaster. Slowly, blow into the wand, aiming bubbles across the top of the hot toaster. What happens to the bubbles as they float over the heated toaster?

Are there other places in your home where you might detect rising hot air by the bubble method?

Project 4

Moon Watch

Discovering the moon's motions

Our moon is always moving in the sky. It takes the moon about 27⅓ days to make one orbit around the Earth. The moon moves across the sky not only because the Earth is turning beneath it, but because the moon is orbiting the Earth.

From your local newspaper, a calendar or an almanac, find out when the next full moon will be. The moon will look full for several days.

Find a window where you can look out in the early evening and see the moon. Use a wide windowsill or move a small table or other surface to the window. Place a piece of cardboard on it to keep it clean. Put some modeling clay on it and mold the clay to be able to hold the cardboard tube from a paper towel roll. The tube will

need to be held in place at an angle at the edge of the sill or table in order for you to look through it.

When the full moon can be seen in the window, look through the tube and move it until the moon is centered in it. Mold the clay around the tube to keep it in place without anyone needing to hold it. Look at a clock. Write down the exact time. Be sure no one in your house touches the tube for the next few days.

The next night, look through the tube again at exactly the exact same time as you did the night before. Is the moon still seen in the middle of the tube?

For the next several nights, look through the tube at exactly the same time. Where is the moon? Is it getting higher in the sky each evening, lower in the sky, or is it in the exact same spot? On paper, draw how much of the moon you see through the tube each night.

Project 5

Double Dipper

Seeing star patterns

To help keep track of the many stars in the sky, the ancient Greeks grouped stars together into patterns. These groups of stars are called constellations. The ancient peoples also gave the constellations names, but today we find it hard to recognize the strange creatures they saw when they looked at the night sky.

The Big Dipper, or The Ladle, in the northern sky is a popular name for a constellation which really does look like a big spoon. The stars that make up the shape of the Big Dipper are part of the constellation the ancients called Ursa Major, which means Great Bear. Can you find the Big Dipper

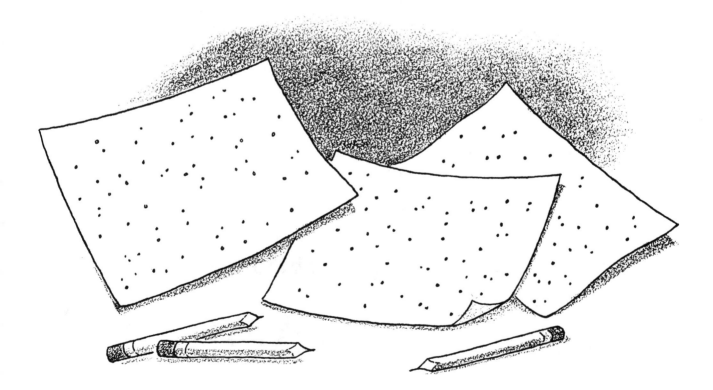

tonight? Can you see other patterns in the sky? Do other people see the same stars that you do? Do you think they see the same patterns in the sky that you do, too?

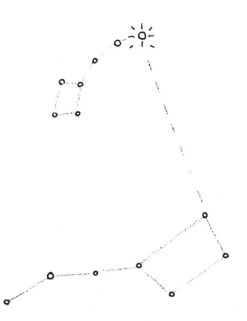

Place some newspaper on a table to protect it from being marked up. Take a sheet of white paper, put it on the newspaper and, with your eyes closed, make about 50 dots all over the paper. To be sure that you are making the dots at random, not in any special pattern, you might want to have a friend slide the paper around a little while you are making the dots. When you are done, take the pencil and make each dot you made a little bigger, so they are easier to see.

Using a copy machine, make 5 copies of your dotted paper.

Taking one of the copies, study the dots. Try to find patterns that look like capital letters of the alphabet and connect some of the dots to make them.

Give one of the other four copies to each of your parents or some of your friends. Don't let them see your copy with the letter shapes on it. Ask them to make as many capital letters as they can by connecting the dots.

Do you think they will see the same patterns in your random dots that you did?

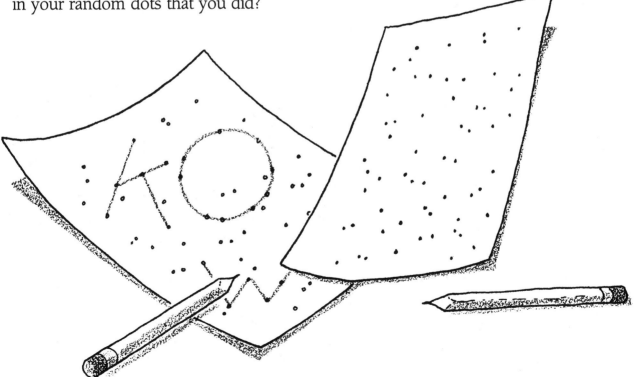

Project 6

Super-Size Surprise

Sunlight from two directions

The diameter of something is the measure of its width from one side to the other. The sun is very far away, but it is so large that its diameter sends a wide path of sunlight to us, from both sides of the sun's diameter and everywhere in between. It even seems as if the light is coming from more than one place, because the wide path of sunlight makes things have more than one shadow.

You need
- pencil
- sheet of typing paper
- book
- ruler
- clothespin or clay
- 2 flashlights

Go outside on a sunny day. Place a sheet of paper on the ground and put a pencil on it. Slowly move the pencil upward. As you raise the pencil above the paper, you will begin to see two shadows. The higher you go, the harder it is to see each shadow. As the light from one side of the sun causes a pencil shadow, it also washes out the pencil shadow caused by the light coming from the other side of the sun's diameter.

Do this little experiment using two flashlights to see how the light coming from each side of the sun is like having two different sources of light. Take the sheet of typing paper and tape it to the side of a book. Open the book a little bit and set it on a table so that the open part faces down. It will look like a movie screen. Use a clothespin or some clay to hold your pencil straight up in the air. Place the pencil about 6 inches (15 cm) in front of the book. Put two flashlights on the table, about 18 inches (45 cm) in front of the book. Turn on one of the flashlights. Point the light at the pencil to make a shadow on the paper screen. Now turn on the second flashlight and point it at the pencil. It will make a shadow of the pencil, too. But see how the light also washes out the first shadow, making it fainter.

Project 7

Cyclops

Two light sources into one

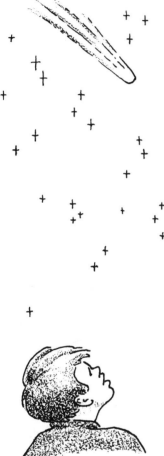

What a shock it was, back in 1609, when Galileo invented the first practical telescope! Through this amazing instrument, people were able to see things in the night sky that they could never see before.

> **You need**
> • a cardboard box, 2 or 3 feet (60–90 cm) high
> • 2 flashlights
> • a clear evening, at dusk

When we look at the sky using only our eyes, almost all we see are just tiny points of light, some brighter, some fainter. But those points of light are really much more than that. With telescopes we can see that one of the points of light is a nearby planet, Saturn, that has rings around it. Big telescopes can see strange cloud-like shapes called nebulae. What looks like just one point of light might actually be two stars, or perhaps even thousands of stars, but without a telescope, we would never know it.

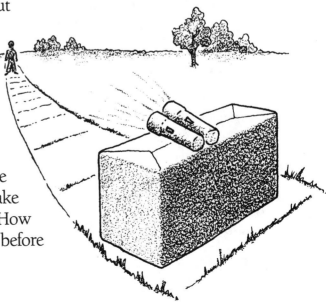

You can prove that it is possible for two sources of light to look like only one. Go outside just before nightfall. Stand a cardboard box on the ground. A sidewalk is good place to set your box. On top of the box place two flashlights side by side. Make sure they are both pointing straight ahead. How far do you have to walk away from the box before the two lights look like just one?

Project 8

High Flyer

Designing paper airplanes for distance

In paper-airplane design, the goal is a plane that will stay in the air a long time before gravity pulls it down. Does wing shape make a difference? What about the material used to make the plane?

Make three paper airplanes using the same design. Instructions for a popular basic design are given on the opposite page, or you can use one of your own. Make one plane using regular paper, one out of aluminum foil, and one out of wax paper. Which plane stays in the air the longest?

You need
- sheet of typing paper
- piece of wax paper
- piece of aluminum foil
- adhesive tape
- paper clips
- tacky clay

Experiment with different airplane designs using the three different types of material. A design that works best for the aluminum plane might not work well for the plane made out of wax paper.

Experiment with different ways of keeping the plane together. Try putting a small bit of flattened tacky clay in the fold at the front. Try placing a paper clip on the bottom of the plane, near its middle. Try putting a piece of light tape on the plane's nose, or across its wingspan.

Do the planes fly better when there is a wind? Should you launch the planes into the wind, or with the wind behind you? Do you get better flights if you just toss the planes easily, or if you throw them harder, trying to make them go farther?

Make a chart of your flight tests and compare the results.

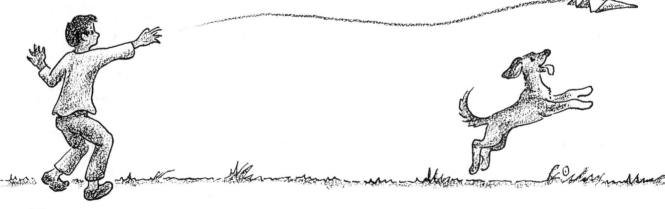

Design for Basic Paper Airplane

1. Fold a sheet of typing paper in half lengthwise and crease it.
2. Open up and flatten the sheet.
3. At one end, fold both corners down, lining edges up with the center crease.
4. Fold each corner edge down again, against the center fold, and crease well. Fold in the sharp point, for safety when tossing.
5. Turn the paper over.
6. Fold the two outer edges back into the creased center line.
7. Fold the plane together and crease all folds well.
8. Bend the wings out into position and test fly your plane.

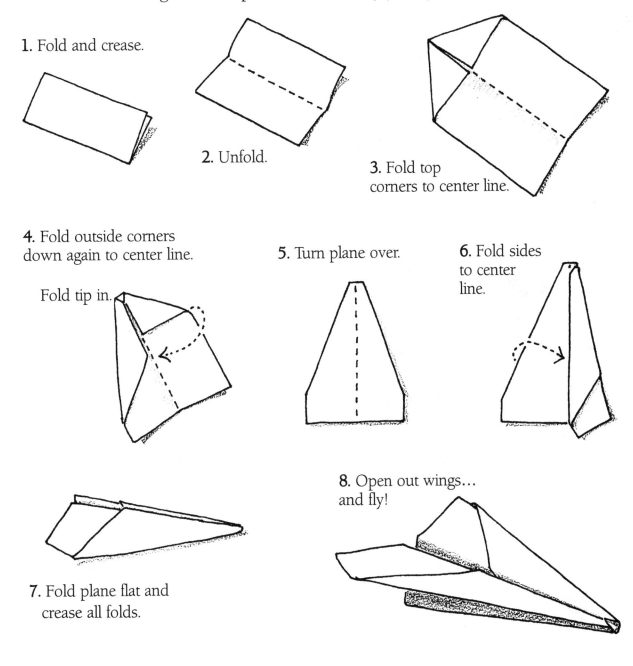

1. Fold and crease.

2. Unfold.

3. Fold top corners to center line.

4. Fold outside corners down again to center line.

Fold tip in.

5. Turn plane over.

6. Fold sides to center line.

7. Fold plane flat and crease all folds.

8. Open out wings... and fly!

Project 9

News Flash

Naming comets

Many comets are discovered by "backyard astronomers," amateurs who enjoy looking at and studying the stars. When a new comet is discovered, it is given the designation of the year and a letter indicating the number of comets that

year. For example, comet 1997b would be the second comet discovered in 1997. Later, the comet is given the name of the person who first discovered it (sometimes two or three people's names are used).

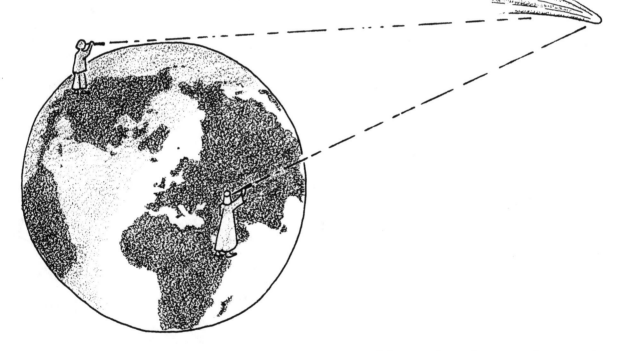

Make believe you discovered a comet. How would you describe it and report its location? What constellation was it in? What star was it near? How bright was it? What time did you discover it? Where were you when you saw it? How long did you watch? What direction was it going? Be as exact as you can.

Write a pretend press release telling the story of your discovery.

Project 10

Overcoming Gravity

Countering one force with another

What is keeping you from floating up into the air right now? It's gravity. All of the planets and the stars have a force, called gravity, that pulls things to them. If you hold something heavy in your hand and hold your arm out straight, you can feel how strong the Earth's gravity is, as it tries to pull your arm downward. But if you know how, you can make an ordinary paper clip defy gravity. Your friends will think you are a magician when they see it floating in midair.

The secret is magnetism, a force that can be stronger than gravity. To defy gravity, tape a strong magnet inside one end of the shoe box. Use construction paper and crayons to decorate the "magic" box, hiding the magnet so your friends can't see it. Stand the shoe box up on the end without the magnet. Tie a piece of thread to a small paper clip. Hold one end of the thread on the inside bottom of the shoe box. Slowly pull the paper clip up towards the magnet, letting the thread out. At the point where the paper clip will stay in the air by itself, tape the section of string touching the bottom to the box. Then pull the clip down, away from the magnet. When your friends come over, slowly lift the paper clip up towards the top of the box and let go when it stands up by itself. Abracadabra!

You need
- shoe box
- thread
- magnet
- construction paper
- adhesive tape
- paper clip
- crayons

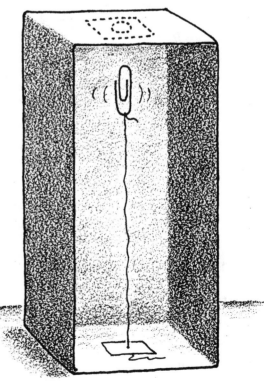

Project 11

A Balanced Diet

Gravity and the balancing point

The attraction objects have for each other is called gravity. Gravity keeps the planets orbiting around the sun, and keeps the moon orbiting around the Earth. The Earth's gravity pulls things down to it.

Have you ever balanced a long pole on your shoulder? Your shoulder was the resting point on which you balanced it. What part did you rest on your shoulder? Was it about at the middle of the pole?

Try balancing a spoon on your finger. Where is the balancing point?

Push the teeth of the two forks together. This new object now has a balancing point that is in midair! You can prove this by pushing a flat stick through the teeth of the forks and resting the middle of the stick on the edge of a coffee cup.

Stand with your back up against a wall and with your heels touching it. Try to bend down and touch your toes while keeping your heels touching the wall. As you start to lean forward, your balancing point changes. It is no longer a point that is over your feet, and you will fall forward.

If an object, like a long pole, is just as heavy on one side as it is the other, the balancing point should be in the middle. But where is the balancing point if one side has more weight?

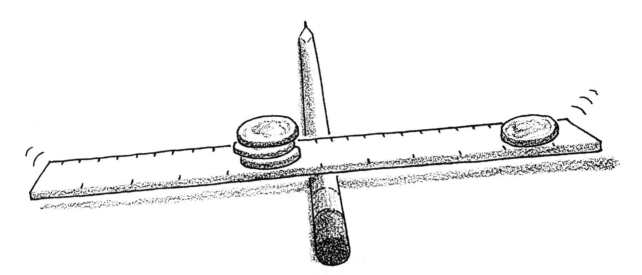

Lay a pencil on a table. Use a pencil which has flat sides to keep it from rolling. Place a ruler on top of it. Balance the ruler as best you can on the pencil. Does it balance at about the mark in the middle? Place a stack of five pennies at a mark to one side. Where on the ruler do you think you would have to place a stack of three pennies to make the ruler balance?

Play a guessing game with your friends. Take turns placing stacks of three, four, five and six pennies at different markings on the ruler and then guess where to put a stack of pennies that has less pennies in it to make the ruler balance.

Project 12

Big Money

Take a coin, cause an eclipse

The sun is very big. Its diameter (the distance across it) is 865,000 miles! The moon is much smaller. Its diameter is only 2,160 miles. There are times when the path of the moon brings it between the sun and the Earth. This causes what is called an eclipse. The moon blocks the sun and the sky goes dark even though it is daytime. How can the tiny moon blot out our view of the giant sun? It happens because things close to you look bigger than when they are farther away.

You can prove this by holding a coin out in front of you at arm's length. Look up at the moon on an evening when the moon is full. Close one eye. Move the nickel between your eye and the moon. Does the nickel blot out the whole moon? (Don't use the sun for this project! *Never* look directly towards the sun or you can hurt your eyes.)

Next, hold a measuring stick vertically (up and down) at arm's length. Look at a telephone pole down the street. Close one eye. Move the ruler between your eye and the telephone pole. Does the ruler blot out the whole telephone pole?

Project 13
Rolling Along
Demonstrating gravity's effect on light

A force is something that causes a change in something else. The force of gravity stops our motion upward when we jump. The gravity of the sun is so strong that it has trapped the Earth and other planets and keeps them all orbiting around it. The gravity of the moon is so strong that it pulls on the Earth's oceans and causes the tides.

You need
- pea-sized steel ball bearing
- strong magnet
- flat table

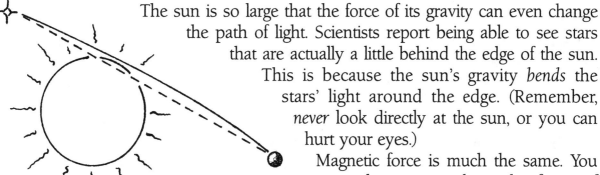

The sun is so large that the force of its gravity can even change the path of light. Scientists report being able to see stars that are actually a little behind the edge of the sun. This is because the sun's gravity *bends* the stars' light around the edge. (Remember, *never* look directly at the sun, or you can hurt your eyes.)

Magnetic force is much the same. You can demonstrate how the force of gravity bends the path of light by using a strong magnet and a steel ball bearing. You might be able to get a ball bearing from your school science teacher, a hobby shop, or a bicycle or machine shop. A TV repair shop is good place to find a strong magnet. An adult could help you remove the magnet from an old speaker.

Roll a ball bearing slowly across a flat tabletop. It should roll in a straight line. Now place the magnet very close to the path where you rolled the ball bearing. Roll it again. Does the path of the ball bearing change as it passes by the magnet?

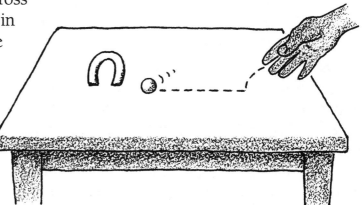

Project 14

Skyworks

All out for meteor spotting

Did you ever see a shooting star? Some people also call them falling stars, but their scientific name is meteors. A meteor is something—a piece of ice or rock—that has been traveling through space and enters the Earth's atmosphere. Some meteors are as tiny as a grain of sand, others are much larger. These meteors are moving so fast that heat caused by friction with the Earth's atmosphere burns them up. That's why we see them in the night sky as bright streaks of light.

You need
- a clear, dark night on one of the evenings listed on chart on opposite page
- bag of dry navy beans
- bowl
- clock or watch

Some meteors are too big to burn up completely, so they hit the Earth's surface. The meteors that hit the Earth are called meteorites. Don't worry about being hit by one. Only about 18 meteorites are found each year, and that includes those that may have fallen ages ago and are only recently discovered.

On any dark, clear night you can usually see a few meteors if you are patient enough and watch closely. At certain times, though, you have a much better chance of seeing lots of them. This is when there is a meteor shower. Some popular meteor showers even have names, and people watch for them at about the same time every year. This is because the Earth moves through the same part of space, and the same clumps of tiny space particles, every year as it orbits the sun.

Scientists aren't sure where all of the meteor shower particles come from. The Taurids shower, which occurs around November 4 every year, is believed to be ice particles from the "tail" of Encke's Comet, and maybe little pieces of the comet head itself. Some meteors could be parts of a broken-up asteroid, or even pieces of the surface of the moon or Mars that were shot up into space during a collision.

On a dark, clear night, go outside and watch for meteors. You may want to put a blanket and pillow on the ground and lie on your back, or lie on an outdoor lounge chair so you can look up at the sky. Dress appropriately for the weather. If the date is close to one of the annual meteor showers (listed on the Annual Meteor Showers chart), take a bag of dry navy beans and bowl outside with you. Watch the sky for

Annual Meteor Showers

Approximate Date	Shower Name
January 3	Quadrantids
April 21	Lyrids
May 4	Eta Aquarids
August 12	Perseids
October 10	Draconids
October 21	Orionids
November 4	Taurids
November 14	Andromedids
November 16	Leonids
December 13	Geminids

one hour. Keep a few beans in your hand. Every time you see a meteor, drop a bean into the bowl. At the end of the hour, count the beans in the bowl to find out how many meteors you saw. By using beans in order to count the meteors that you see, instead of using a pencil and paper, you don't have to take your eyes off the sky or use any light.

Learn more about meteors and meteorites at your local library or science center.

Project 15

Marble Slide

Trajectory trials

The path an object takes as it travels through the air is called its trajectory. The Earth's gravity pulls on everything. If you throw an object, it will not go straight. Soon it falls to the ground. The harder you throw it, the farther it will go before it hits the ground, but it will still hit the ground eventually. It is gravity that keeps you from being able to throw a baseball into space, no matter how good you can throw.

You need
- modeling clay
- tube from a paper towel roll
- marble
- several sheets of typing paper
- adhesive tape
- pencil
- cardboard
- an uncarpeted floor under the table

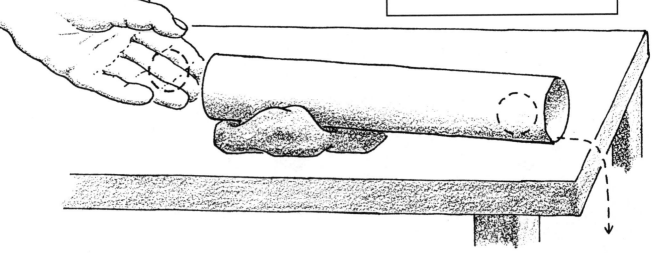

Let's play a guessing game about the trajectory of a marble rolling off a table. Put some cardboard on a table to protect it. Place a mound of modeling clay on the cardboard and make a marble slide by laying the tube against the mound so that the lower end is just slightly off the table. The slope or angle of the tube slide should be very small, that is, the higher end of the tube only a little higher than the lower end.

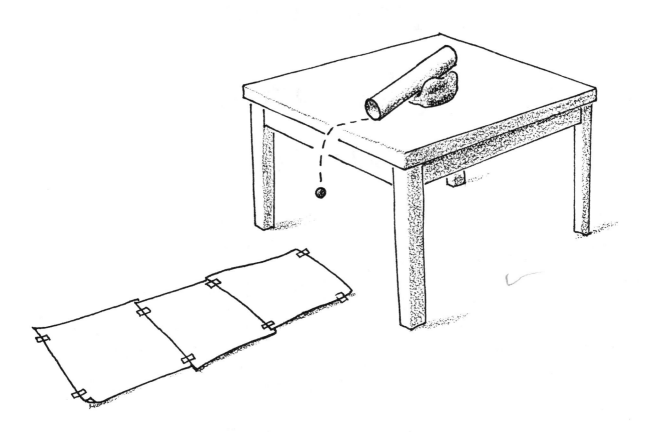

Take three or four sheets of typing paper and tape them together, end to end, making one long piece of paper a yard or so long (90 cm). Put the paper on the floor under the edge of the table below the marble slide. Tape the paper to the floor so it won't move.

Hold a marble at the raised end of the slide. Let it go. (Don't push it at all. Let the marble roll on its own.) As the marble rolls off the edge of the table, watch where it hits the floor. Mark the landing spot on the paper with a pencil.

Next, add a little more modeling clay to raise the end of the marble slide higher. Guess where the marble will hit the floor now. Mark the spot on the paper where you think it will land. Gravity will still pull the marble downward, the same as before, but this time the marble will be traveling faster when it rolls off the end of the table. Do you think the marble will move farther away from the table before gravity causes it to hit the paper?

Try raising and lowering the higher end of the paper towel slide. You and your friends can guess where the marble will land each time. Whoever is closest is the winner.

Does the distance get bigger as the marble slide gets higher?

Project 16

Ski Jump

Universal pull of gravity

The pull of the Earth's gravity is the same for everything on its surface. But what if you were to *drop* a marble, and at the same time *throw* a second marble from the same height? Would that make a difference, or would both marbles hit the floor at the same time?

You know, of course, that the thrown marble would travel farther away from you, and that gravity would still pull it down, just the same as the marble that was dropped. But this project will prove that even though an object is moving fast

parallel to the ground (sideways, not up and down), gravity will make it hit the ground at the same time as a marble simply dropped from the same height.

You will need a table on an uncarpeted, bare floor. Place some cardboard on the table, to keep it clean, and put two mounds of modeling clay on the cardboard. Make one mound only about 1 inch (3 cm) high and the other mound about 6 or 7 inches (15–18 cm) high. Push two rulers into one end of the short mound, to form a "V" shape (measuring edge inward). This will make a ramp for a marble to run down. Using two more rulers, make another "V" ramp and set it on the higher clay mound. Mold the clay around the rulers to keep them in place.

You now have two marble ramps, one with a low slope and one with a high slope. Place the low end of the ramps about one inch from the edge of the table.

One marble should be moving more slowly, when it falls from the edge of the table, than the other one from the higher ramp. Listen and your ears will tell you if both marbles hit the floor at the same time. If they do, you will hear the sound of them landing together. If you hear two separate sounds, then the marbles didn't hit at the same time.

In order for the results to be accurate, both marbles must leave the edge of the table at the exact same time. The marble on the low-sloped ramp will have to start farther up the ramp than the marble on the high-sloped ramp. You will have to

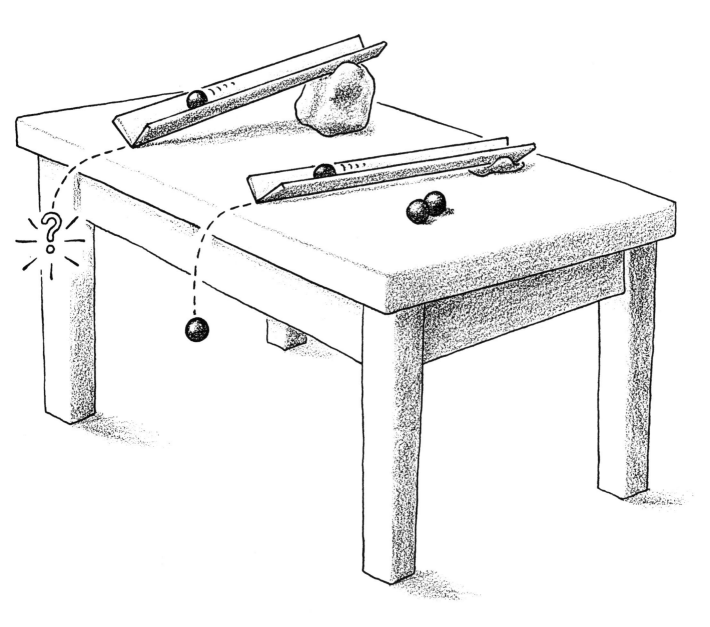

experiment letting go of both marbles at different points on the rulers. Use the measurements marked on the rulers as your guides. When you let go of the marbles, listen for the click sound that they make when they hit the tabletop. If you hear more than one sound, then they did not hit the table at the same time, and you will need to change the starting position of one of the marbles.

Once you get both marbles to leave the edge of the table at the same time, listen for the sound of them hitting the floor at the same time. Both marbles will fall the same distance in the same amount of time, but the one moving faster will have traveled farther from the table.

Once you are satisfied with the results of your same-size marble experiments, do the same test using two different-size marbles and compare your results. Does the size of the marbles used count?

Project 17

Paper Moon

Creating a moonscape

Unlike Earth, the moon has no atmosphere. There's no air or water on the moon, so there's no weather or erosion there. Because of these differences, the surface of the moon does not look like that of the Earth.

Create a model showing the different features of the moon. Some of the features of your moonscape should include seas, craters, rays, rills, domes and scarps.

To make your lunar model, turn a large bowl upside down and cover it with wax paper. Tape the wax paper together and to the bowl to protect it as you form your lunar landscape. The bowl is the mold for the base of your papier-mâché moon.

To make the papier-mâché base, make a sticky paste of flour and water. Mix it

You need
- 2 large bowls
- wax paper
- adhesive tape
- flour
- water
- strips of newspaper
- modeling clay
- flat stick
- toothpick

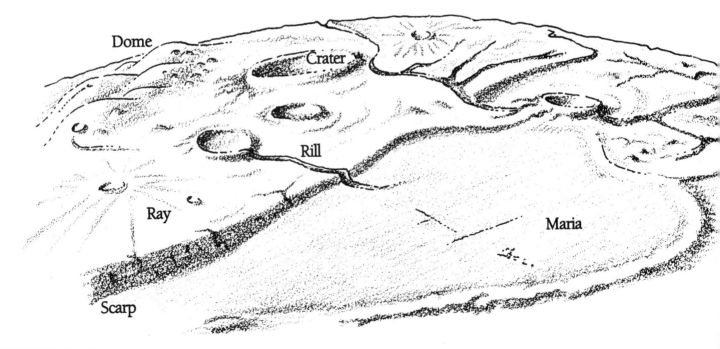

34

until the paste is smooth and easy to work with. Add flour or water if it seems too wet or too dry. Next, tear short strips of newspaper, about 1 inch (3 cm) wide, and dip them in the mixture. Using a crisscross pattern, place the coated papier-mâché strips over the whole bowl. Let this covering dry for a few days, then add another layer of papier-mâché and let it dry for several more days.

Instead of using only flour and water, salt can be used in the mixture, or the paper strips can be glued onto the wax-paper-covered bowl to make the base for the lunar landscape.

When dry, cover the whole dome with a layer of modeling clay. Use a flat stick and a toothpick to help you form the different features. Your own Moonscape does not have to be an exact model of Earth's moon. It can just represent the different physical features that are found on the moon.

Lunar Topography

Maria, smooth lunar "seas" that we see from Earth, are large dark plains. Although they are called seas, even on lunar maps, they are not seas at all because there is no water on the moon.

Craters are round low areas surrounded by raised walls, like mountains, forming a circle or ring. Some lunar craters are thousands of miles across and thousands of feet deep.

Rays we see are bright streaks that extend out from the middle of some of the lunar craters. The largest rays can be seen coming from the crater Tycho.

Rills are long narrow trenches. Some are very deep. From Earth they look like winding rivers some hundreds of miles long.

Domes on the moon are smooth, gently sloping, low mounds, like sand dunes, that don't cast any shadows. Most are between 3 and 12 miles (5–20 km) across.

Scarps are lunar cliffs. They may be as little as a couple of feet (65 cm) to thousands of feet high.

Project 18

Over & Under

Air movement and air pressure

When you put one end of a straw in your mouth and the other end in a glass of milk or soda can in order to drink, and then suck on it, the liquid travels up the straw. The reason that happens is lower air pressure. How do you know that?

If you put a second straw in your mouth, and *don't* put the other end into the drink, you will no longer be able to drink it. You won't be able to lower the air pressure in your mouth by

sucking, because air will come in through the second straw. But, pinch the end of the second straw closed, and you are suddenly able to drink the milk or soda again! (Try it and prove it to yourself if you like.)

In addition to helping you use a straw to drink, lower air pressure plays a very important part in keeping airplanes up. How? Let's put on a demonstration.

Push one thumbtack into each side of a wooden doorway, maybe the doorway to your bedroom, at about waist height. Next, tie a string to one thumbtack, stretch the string tightly across the doorway and tie it to the thumbtack on the other side.

Take a strip of paper about an inch (2.5 cm) wide by 11 or 12 inches (30 cm) long. Fold about a half inch (1 cm) of the end of the paper strip over the string and secure it with a staple or small piece of tape. The loop should be loose enough so the paper moves freely on the string. Gravity will make the paper hang down.

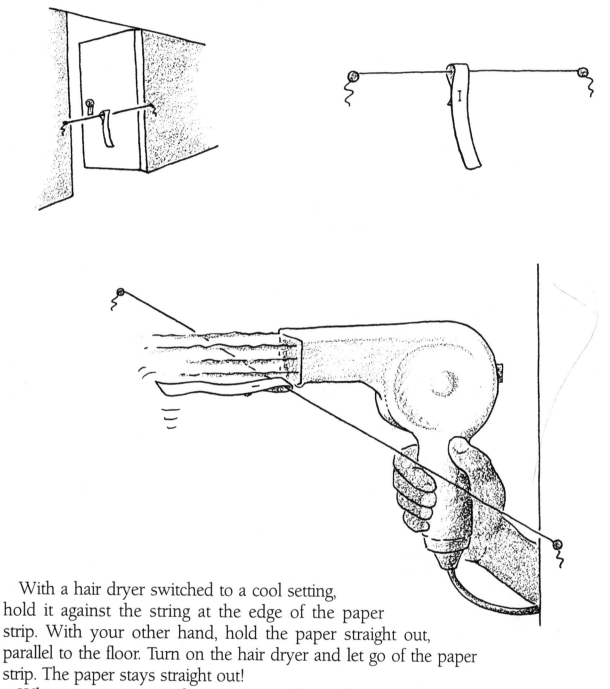

With a hair dryer switched to a cool setting, hold it against the string at the edge of the paper strip. With your other hand, hold the paper straight out, parallel to the floor. Turn on the hair dryer and let go of the paper strip. The paper stays straight out!

When air moves very fast across a surface, it lowers the air pressure there. As long as the fast-moving air blows along the top of the paper strip, it will stay in position. The strip is being held there, sandwiched by the push of the higher air pressure above and below it.

Project 19

Drop Zone

Parachute design

Sailors have life preservers to use in an emergency; pilots keep their parachutes handy. When you run and fall, the pull of gravity can make you skin your knee. The higher you are when you start falling, like from a chair or ladder, the faster and harder you fall. When a plane is in trouble, using a parachute can save the pilot's life. Parachutes are also used to slow the fall of air-dropped food and supplies to remote places and to bring space capsules safely back to Earth.

A parachute uses air resistance that stops a falling object from landing so hard. It's called a soft landing. What affects air resistance? Can it be controlled?

The suspension lines tied between the parachute and the harness that a person wears are called shrouds. Is the length of these shroud lines important in the parachute's design? Make two parachutes, having different shroud lengths, and compare their ability to slow an object's fall.

Ask an adult to help you find an old T-shirt, pillow case or bed sheet and cut two 10-inch-square (26-cm) pieces of cloth for the parachutes. (You won't want to cut up good material, and you may need to use extra-sharp scissors to cut the cloth.) Tie four pieces of thread about 6 inches (15 cm) long to a small (¼-inch/½-cm) nut. Tie one end of each piece of string to a corner of a cloth square.

Tie four pieces of thread 12 inches (30 cm) long to another small nut. Tie one end of each piece of thread to a corner of a cloth square.

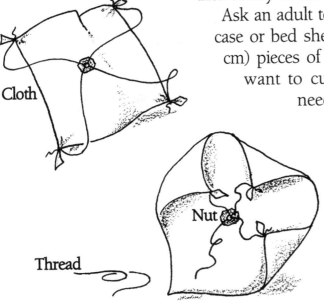

Cloth

Nut

Thread

Stand where you can drop the parachutes from a height, such as off the side of a porch or flight of stairs. With one in each hand, hold the two parachutes by pinching the center of the cloths, letting the nuts hang down underneath. Stretch your arms out and let go of both parachutes at the same time.

Do they land on the ground at the same time? If not, which one stays in the air the longest, the one with the 4-inch (10-cm) shroud lines or the one with the 10-inch (26-cm) lines?

Project 20
Cool Air Lift
What keeps airplanes up?

Why are airplane wings shaped the way they are? The curve of the wing top forces the air moving over it to travel farther then the air passing underneath, so the air has to move faster. When that happens, it lowers the air pressure above the wing and gives the plane what is known as lift.

You need
- paper towel tube
- pencil with flat sides
- ruler
- hair dryer
- table
- scissors
- 2 books of equal thickness

Ask an adult to cut a paper-towel tube in half, then lengthwise, to make two short curved pieces. Push down a little along one side of the length of one tube to flatten it slightly and give it an airplane-wing shape. One side of the tubing will have more curve: this will be the front. The flatter side, with less curve, will be the back.

Lay two books of the same thickness near the edge of a table. Place them about three inches (7–8 cm) apart and lay a pencil across them, from one to the other. Use a pencil with flat sides to keep it from rolling.

Put the paper-towel tube wing on the side of a ruler, lined up with the end. Place the ruler and wing on the pencil so that it balances like a seesaw. The end of the ruler with the wing on it should hang out over the edge of the table.

Using a hair dryer on a cool setting, blow air at the curved, front edge of the wing. The air pressure will be lower above the wing as the fast-moving air travels up and around it, and the seesaw balance will begin to tip. Which end rises?

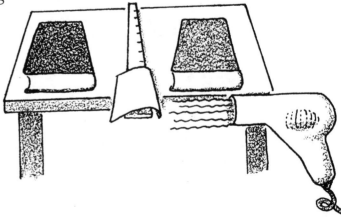

Project 21

Move Over!

Motion beats the power of gravity

You can throw a ball straight up—but not very far. Gravity pulls it down. But your throwing motion does overcome gravity for a short while.

It is possible, however, for motion to overcome gravity. Tie three of the small (¼-inch/½-cm) nuts onto the end of a two-foot long (60-cm) piece of string. Pass the other end of the string through the hole of an empty thread spool. Tie one small nut onto that other end of the string. For safety's

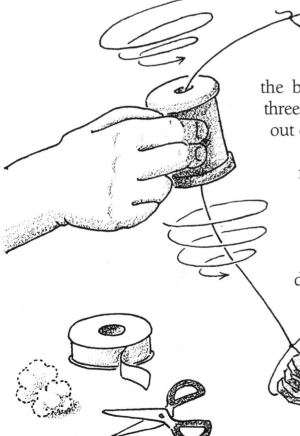

sake, cover the nuts with some cotton and secure with tape.

Hold the spool so that the string is hanging, with the three nuts at the bottom. Gravity is, of course, pulling the three nuts down. Pull several inches of string up out of the top of the spool.

Now, slowly move the spool in a circular motion to swing the upper nut around. The faster you move the spool, swinging the upper nut, the higher the string will come out of the spool, lifting the three nuts on the other end. Be careful as the string is drawn up, making larger and larger circles, so that you are not hit by the swinging nut.

It is the action of centrifugal force that is pulling the revolving nut away from the center of the spool and overcoming gravity's pull on the other three nuts.

Project 22

Stellar Performance

The night sky as the Earth turns

As the Earth turns, the stars in the sky above seem to be moving. How fast? Let's track it.

Place a piece of thread straight across the middle of one end opening of a paper-towel tube and tape it in place. Now tape another piece of thread across the opening, but at a 90-degree angle so that the threads cross in the center. The "X" will help you position a star in your viewfinder.

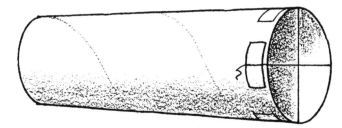

On a clear night, go outside and pick a bright star. Place the viewfinder on a support and point it at the star. The end with the thread cross-hairs should be towards the star. Position your viewfinder so that the star you picked appears in the exact center of the tube,

right where the two threads cross. Use modeling clay to fix the viewfinder in position. Look at a clock and write down the time.

Once every minute, look through your viewfinder and see if the star has moved. On your paper, draw what you see in the viewfinder and note the time. How long does it take for you to notice that the star is no longer positioned at the X point? How long before the star is completely out of sight in the viewfinder?

Now pick a different star and repeat the experiment. Did it take the same amount of time for this star to travel out of sight in your viewfinder?

Project 23

Sun Day News

The changing length of day and night

Because the Earth turns completely around every twenty-four hours, the sun seems to rise and set once each day. The time between sunrise and sunset is called length of day. Does it change from day to day and month to month? How about the moon? Does the time between moonrise and moonset change each day? How does it compare to the time of sunrise and sunset?

You need
- daily newspaper for 7 days
- paper
- pencil

Buy a newspaper that lists the times of sunrise and sunset, and moonrise and moonset, each day. Get the paper every day for seven days in a row. Make up a chart showing the time of sunrise and sunset for each day. Calculate the length of day and fill in your chart with the times. Study your chart. Is the length of day getting longer or shorter?

As the Earth travels around the sun, there are two times during the year when day and night are equal in length around the world. This time is called equinox. The vernal (spring) equinox happens around March 20. The autumnal equinox happens around September 22. On the equinoxes, the length of day and night are each twelve hours long, since there are 24 hours in a day.

During the year, there's a time when the length of day is longest, and a time exactly opposite when the length of day is the shortest—when the sun rises late and goes to bed early. The shortest day is called the winter solstice. The longest day is called the summer solstice. In the Northern Hemisphere, the winter solstice happens around December 21. It is officially the first day of winter. The summer solstice happens around June 20, the first day of summer. Look at your chart. Is the length of day getting longer or shorter? According to your chart, are you heading towards the winter solstice or the summer solstice?

Project 24

Two Bright

Light pollution

Most of us have heard about air pollution, but astronomers and others who enjoy studying the night sky are also aware of light pollution. Light pollution is when the light from homes and businesses, signs, street lamps, neon lights, and other artificial sources "wash out" the dark sky, preventing us from seeing the fainter stars.

Show how bright light can actually keep you from seeing details by washing out your vision.

On a piece of white poster board, clearly write a number of letters of the alphabet, like an eye doctor's testing chart with big letters at the top, a line of smaller letters underneath, and even smaller letters in each line farther down. Start with letters big enough to see from about 20 feet (8 m) away.

On a dark night, have an adult stand in front of an automobile, hold up the poster board, and shine a flashlight on it. Stand facing the automobile, but about 20 feet (8 m) away, and read as many letters as you can.

Next, have the adult turn on the headlights of the automobile behind the poster board. Even though the flashlight is still trained on it, how many letters can you read now, with the headlights on?

You need
- automobile and help of adult
- flashlight
- sheet of white poster board
- black marker
- a dark evening

Project 25

Tomorrow's Astronauts

Visit to a pretend planet

Choose a planet other than the Earth. In order from our sun, they are Mercury and Venus, closer to the sun, and Mars, Jupiter, Saturn, Uranus, Neptune and Pluto, farther away than we are. Go to the library, use your own encyclopedia and reference books, or search the Internet. Learn as much as you can about the planet you choose. Write down where you got each of your facts.

Write a script for a skit about what it would be like to travel in a spaceship and land on that planet. Hypothesize what you and your crew would see and feel, based on what you learned in your research. Would you have trouble breathing? Finding food and water? Staying warm? Moving around? How many moons do you see in the sky? How big are they and how do they move? What does the landscape around you look like? What does the Earth look like to you when you are standing on your planet's surface? Can you see the Earth at all? Does your planet revolve? How long are the days and nights there? Is there anything of value on the planet, such as ore that could be mined?

With some friends, or at school, use cardboard and other arts-and-crafts materials to make a ship, scenery and props for your skit. Make spacesuits and other costumes (the planet's native life forms?) for the actors to wear.

If you have and can use a video camera, it might be nice to record the skit for a science fair presentation.

Project 26
Sun Trek

Tracking the sun's movement

Every day, as the Earth turns on its axis, the sun seems to move across the sky. To safely track this movement over several hours (never look directly at the sun or you can damage your eyes), we will construct and use a special charting box.

Remove the top flaps from a cardboard box about 2 feet (60 cm) square. Set the box on its side with the opening facing you. Ask an adult to help cut a small hole, a few inches wide, in the top side of the box, near the middle. Place a piece of thin poster board over the hole, closing it up, and tape it in place. Very carefully, make a sharp, tiny hole in the center of the poster board with a safety pin or needle, so that it also passes through the hole in the side of the box.

You need
- cardboard box
- thin poster board
- adhesive tape
- safety pin
- brick
- a sunny day
- scissors
- unlined white paper
- clock
- pencil
- adult with penknife

Inside the box, lay a sheet of white paper on the bottom and tape it down.

Take the box outside on a sunny day. Point the top of the box towards the sun. Use a brick or flat board to tilt the box, if the sun is not directly overhead. A small white dot of sunlight will shine through the pinhole onto the paper. With a pencil, mark the spot on the paper where the light hits. Look at a clock and write the time next to the spot. Every half hour, mark the spot where the sunlight hits and write down the time.

After several hours, remove the paper and study your marks. It may seem that the marks were tracking the sun, but since the sun does not move, it is actually the Earth's movement that was tracked.

Project 27

I Am a Sundial

Telling time from the sun

On a sunny day, unless the sun is directly over your head, your body casts a shadow. Sometimes your shadow is short and sometimes it's long. Did you know that that fact can tell you the time?

Take poster boards and tape them end to end to make a large sheet about 3 by 8 feet (100 x 250 cm).

At 1 p.m. on a sunny afternoon, stand outside with your back to the sun. Lay the poster board sheet down on the ground. Stand with the toes of your shoes just touching one edge, so you cast a shadow onto the boards. Have a friend draw the outline of your shadow with a dark crayon or marker. Write the time next to the outline.

At 2 o'clock, in the same place, have your friend draw your shadow again. Write "2 p.m." by the outline. At 3, 4 and 5 o'clock, have your shadow drawn again, marking the time of day. Did your shadow grow longer as the time passed? That means your shadow gets longer as the Earth turns away from the sun.

The next afternoon, take your poster-board "shadow map" outside and stand with your back to the sun. With the map on the ground at your feet and your feet against the boards as before, look at the shadow you cast. Without a clock, about what time is it? You can tell by comparing your shadow now to your outlines from the day before. What do you suppose happens to your shadow in the morning?

Get information on sundials and how they work, then bring your human sundial shadow-map project to school to share with your class.

Project 28
Sunny Spotlight
The art of spreading light

Although it may seem that way, it isn't hotter in the summer because the Earth is closer to the sun, and colder in the winter because it is farther away. The seasonal changes from winter, to spring, to summer, to autumn are caused by the Earth's movement around the sun and the fact that the Earth is tilted about 23 degrees, instead of straight up and down like a top. This changes the angle at which sunlight hits the surface of the

You need
- clipboard
- sheet of unlined paper
- flashlight
- hardback book
- pencil

Earth, as it makes its one-year journey around the sun. The Northern Hemisphere gets more sunlight when the Earth is tipped towards the sun, so it is hotter (summer in the Northern Hemisphere). At the same time, the Southern Hemisphere is tilted at an angle away from the sun. The sunlight spreads out more thinly over a greater area there, so it is colder (winter in the Southern Hemisphere).

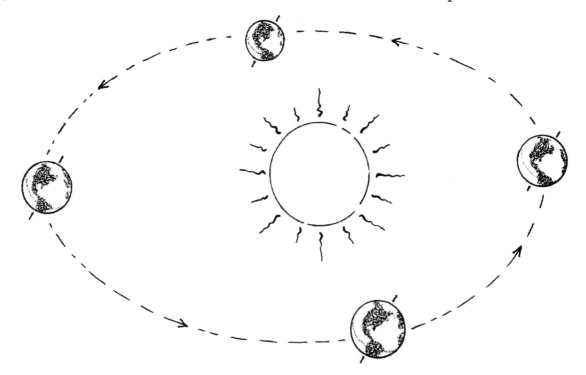

Light rays are strongest when they hit straight on. It is usually hotter at noon, when the sun is right overhead, than in the early morning or late evening. Light is weakest when rays hit a surface on an angle, because the light is forced to spread out and cover more of the surface. Show how light spreads out when it hits a surface tilted at an angle to the light source.

Place a hardback book on a table and open it slightly so it will stand up. Turn a flashlight on and set it on top of the book.

Clip a sheet of unlined white paper onto a clipboard. Hold the clipboard straight up and down in front of the flashlight. With a pencil, draw an outline around the circle of light on the paper.

Now tilt the clipboard away from the flashlight. Draw an outline around the oval of light on the paper.

Compare the circle and the oval. Did the light spread out more when the clipboard was tilted away from the light source?

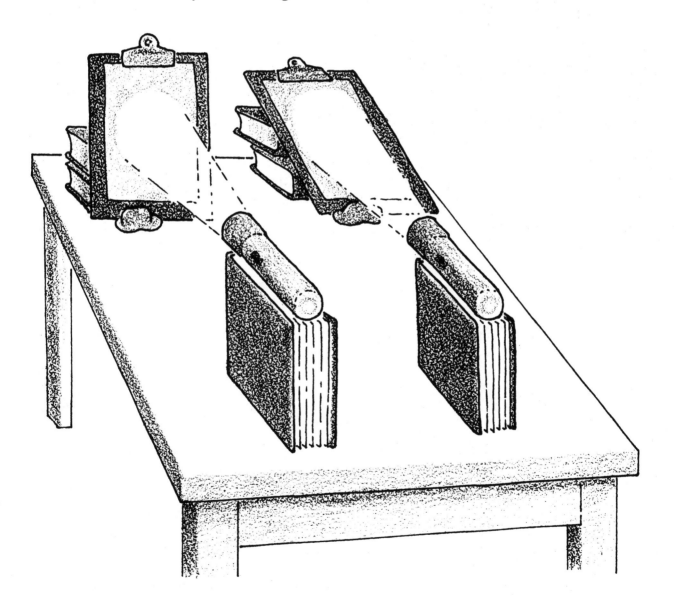

Project 29

Once Around the Sun

Comparing planetary years

How long is a year? That depends on which planet you are on. The time it takes for the Earth to make one orbit around the sun is one Earth year. The orbits of the different planets are larger the farther away they are from the sun, so it takes them a longer time to go once around the sun. Mercury and Venus are closer to the sun than the Earth is, so a year on those planets is shorter than one Earth year.

You need
• 9 different colors of yarn
• scissors
• masking tape
• a long wall
• research books
• paper and pencil

Research how long it takes each of the nine planets in our solar system to go once around the sun. Find the length of each planet's year in Earth time; for example, it takes Mercury only about 88 Earth days to complete its circle around the sun, while Pluto takes about 247½ Earth years!

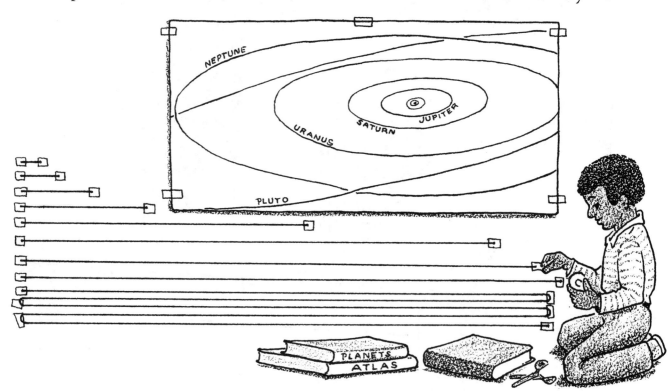

When you've finished, change the time to months. Mercury, then, would take 3 months, Earth would take 12 months and Pluto 2,970 months.

Gather nine different colors of yarn. Choose a color for each planet. The yarn will represent the length of time it takes for that planet to go around the sun once. One inch, or one centimeter, can represent one month. By that measurement, the length of yarn for Mercury's orbit will be 3 inches or centimeters, Earth's will be 12 and Pluto's will be 2,970!

Near a corner of a long wall, tape one end of each piece of yarn. Keep the yarn pieces separate and straight, and tape up the other ends. Some pieces of yarn, especially the one representing Pluto's year, will be so long you will have to fold them back and forth *several times* along the wall. (If wall space is limited, use smaller measurements. For example, let the length of Mercury's year, 3 months, equal ½ inch, ½ centimeter, etc.)

Label each yarn strand by writing down the name of the planet and the length of its year in Earth time. Adding each planet's symbol (the drawings that represent them) and other information you learn about the planets in our Solar System will make your project even better.

Planets + Symbols

o Mercury ☿

O Venus ♀

O Earth ⊕

o Mars ♂

Jupiter ♃

Saturn ♄

Uranus ♅

Neptune ♆

o Pluto ♇

Project 30

Just Add Air

Making environmental changes

There are aircraft known as heavier-than-air (airplanes, helicopters, gliders) and those that are lighter than air (balloons, blimps). Balloons that carry people, weather instruments or other loads rise because the total weight of the gas in the balloon, the balloon itself, the passengers and the basket is still less than the weight of the air that would take up the same amount of space.

We live at the bottom of an ocean of air. Air and water behave much the same way. We can

You need
- an adult with a drill
- plastic soda bottle with screw cap
- water-filled tub or large pail
- small pebbles or stones
- 3 feet (90 cm) of plastic aquarium tubing
- rubber band

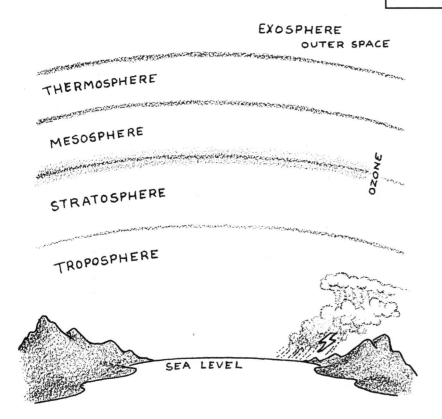

EXOSPHERE
OUTER SPACE

THERMOSPHERE

MESOSPHERE

OZONE

STRATOSPHERE

TROPOSPHERE

SEA LEVEL

demonstrate the lighter-than-air idea by using a bottle in a bathtub full of water.

Have an adult drill three small holes, each about ¼ inch (7 mm) in diameter, into an empty, plastic soda bottle (16/20 ounce or half liter). The drilled holes need to be about two inches (5 cm) or so up from the bottom of the bottle.

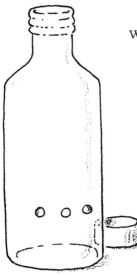

Fill a tub or pail with water. Push the bottle into the water so that the water level is just above the three holes, letting water go into the bottle.

The bottle will float.

Drop a few small pebbles into the bottom of the plastic soda bottle. Add pebbles until the bottle sinks. Screw the cap on the bottle.

Take one end of the piece of plastic tubing and stick it into the bottle through one of the small holes. Bending the end upward, push it towards the inside top of the bottle. Place a rubber band around the bottle to hold the tube in place. Next, blow into the tube.

When you blow through the tube and into the bottle, the air pushes water out of the holes and replaces it. The air inside the bottle weighs less than the atmosphere outside the bottle (water), so the bottle rises. You can make the bottle rise and fall in the water by blowing air in or letting air out of the bottle.

Project 31

Drag On

Air's resistance to motion

"Drag" is a word used by people in aviation. It means the resistance of air to the forward motion of an aircraft. As an object tries to move faster through the air, the air tries to slow it down.

You need
• 3 sheets of typing paper

Take three sheets of regular typing paper. Hold your hand out at arm's length, with your palm upward. Lay a piece of paper flat on your hand. Pull your hand away. Watch how slowly the paper falls to the floor.

Lightly crumple another piece of paper into a ball. Hold it out at arm's length and drop it. Did the ball of paper push through the air and fall faster?

Make a paper airplane. Hold it out with its nose pointing towards the floor. Let it go.

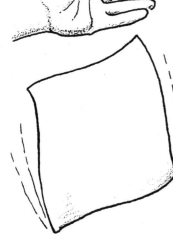
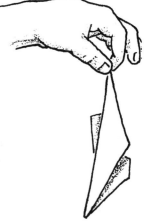

Which of the three sheets of paper fell the fastest (had the least drag slowing it down)?

Look at the designs of different cars and airplanes. How do their shapes reduce drag and allow them to move faster through the air? How can you use that information the next time you take part in a race?

Project 32

No Strings

Balancing with pressures

It might look like magic to suspend a Ping-Pong ball in midair, without anything touching it, but it's not. The secret is balancing air push and pressure, and, voilà! The ball floats!

Place a hair dryer on a table and point it so the flow of air will go straight up. Several hardbound books will hold the dryer in place. Set the hair dryer to the fastest speed but the coolest position and turn it on. Gently place a Ping-Pong ball in the middle of the air column from the dryer. Let go of the ball, and it will stay in place, hovering over the hair dryer as if by magic.

You need
- hair dryer
- several hardbound books
- Ping-Pong ball
- stiff cardboard about 5 or 6 inches (12 or 15 cm) square
- table

go of the ball, and it will stay in place, hovering over the hair dryer as if by magic.

Now, take a piece of stiff cardboard or poster board. Holding the stiff board upright, slowly move it towards the floating ball. As the board nears the ball, the ball will start to move towards the cardboard. In order to squeeze between the board and ball, the moving air is forced to speed up. When the air moves faster, it causes a drop in air pressure, so the ball is pushed by higher air pressure in that direction. This is what happens to airplanes in flight. Pilots have to be ready to adjust for air pressure differences caused by weather or, if they are flying low, by differences in the landscape.

Can you make the ball go higher by making the air from the dryer move even faster? Try covering part, half or more of the hair dryer opening with a piece of cardboard and see what happens.

Project 33

Wane, Wane, Go Away

Charting the phases of the moon

As the nights go by, the moon seems to change shape. At times, only a thin curved piece, a "crescent," is visible. It appears to grow bigger each day until it becomes a round, brightly lit disc. Then it starts to disappear, with less and less of the moon being seen. Finally, it is only a crescent again, and then the moon vanishes altogether.

You need
- one month
- paper and pencil

These changes in the appearance of the moon are called "phases." It takes a little over 28 days for the moon to go through its pattern of changes and start over again. The moon, of course, doesn't really change shape. It is always round. It's the light from the sun, shining on the moon, that causes the changes we see. It is true

---

The Lunar Phases

Astronomers have named several stages of the moon's phases. A "New Moon" is when you can't see it at all. A "Full Moon" is a completely lit moon. If you take the new, full, and two phases in between (which make four phases), you can call a halfway lit moon the "first quarter" and "last quarter" phases. In between those times are "crescent" phases, when only a small curved piece is lit, and "gibbous" phases, when all *but* a small curved piece is lit and the moon looks like a football.

When the crescent and gibbous phases are working towards a Full Moon stage, they are said to be "waxing," or building up. When the crescent and gibbous phases are heading towards a New Moon, it is called "waning." (A wane, wane moon soon "goes away.")

---

that the sun is always shining on the moon, but we here on Earth can only see the lit side that's facing us. We can't see the dark side against the dark sky.

Every evening for a month, look at the moon and draw what you see. Don't worry about skipping a night if you can't watch, or when the sky is overcast or it is raining. The changes in the moon's phases happen slowly, and you won't miss much by not watching one night.

When you have completed your moon chart for a month, you can use it as a guide. Then, when you look at the moon, you will be able to tell which part of the cycle it is in, and predict if it is heading towards a "Full Moon" or a "New Moon."

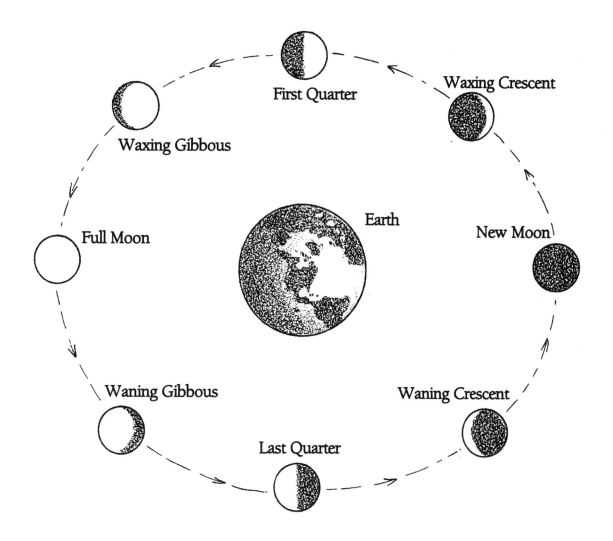

Project 34

Tilt!

Our solar system's leaning planets

The sun's planets orbit it, moving roughly along the same flat plane, except for Pluto which orbits slightly above it. This plane is an imaginary line that can be drawn through two points on the Earth's orbit; this so-called orbital plane extends across and out past all the planets. Think of the sun as being in the middle of a gigantic plate, and all the planets placed on the flat plate, or plane, around it.

If you were to also draw an imaginary line through the North and South Poles of a planet (the axis on which a planet turns), you would find that some planets are tilted. The axis isn't perpendicular (90 degrees) to the plane of the orbit. In other words, the planets are not spinning straight up; they are not as a book standing up on a table is perpendicular to it.

The Earth, for example, is tilted at about 23 degrees from the perpendicular to its orbit. Because the Earth is tilted, we have the changing of the seasons (winter, spring, summer and fall). Pluto has a 17-degree tilt. Uranus is really weird, spinning on its side at a 98-degree angle!

Make nine balls out of modeling clay, one for each planet in our solar system. You may make some balls bigger than the others, since the planets are different sizes, but the balls don't have to be made to scale. Push a pencil through the middle of each

You need
- 9 pencils
- modeling clay
- toothpicks
- paper or index cards
- protractor
- research books
- adhesive tape
- hardbound book

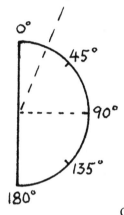

ball. This will represent the planet's axis, the imaginary line around which the planet spins.

Write the name of each planet on small pieces of paper or cards that you can bend and stand in front of each clay model. Research the angle of tilt for each planet and put that information on the cards.

Using adhesive tape, stick a protractor onto the side of a tabletop, so that the 90 degree mark is in line with the table's surface (see illustration) and the 0 degree mark is straight up. Set a clay ball next to the protractor. Turn the ball so that the pencil is at about the angle the planet is tilted. Push three toothpicks into the bottom of the ball, making a set of three (tripod) legs for it to stand on. Do this for each of the nine planets.

When you set the model planets on a table, put Pluto up on a book to raise it above the plane of the surface. This will represent the number of degrees that Pluto is above the plane of the solar system.

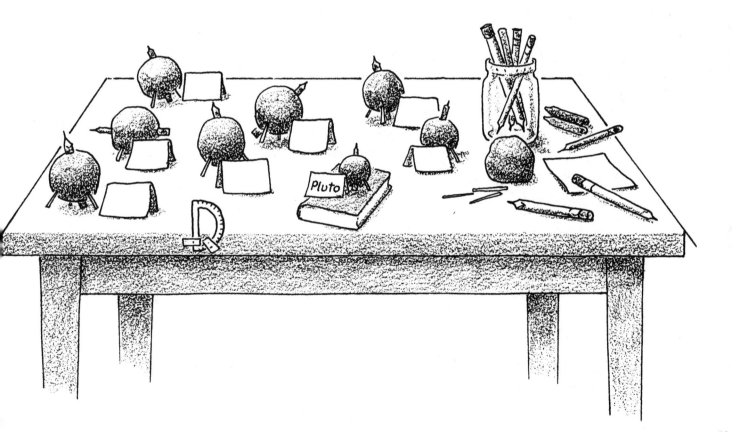

Project 35

Rings in the Sky

A motion study of Saturn's rings

A number of planets have rings encircling them, but the most spectacular by far are those around Saturn. It's thought that Saturn's rings are made up of an almost infinite number of ice crystals and ice-covered particles. Some of the particles are as small as a grain of sand and others are as big as a house.

Saturn is tilted on its axis (see Project 34) about 28 degrees and takes almost 30 Earth years (see Project 29) to complete one orbit around the sun. As the Earth and Saturn orbit the sun, we are able to see Saturn from different angles. Sometimes, when the rings are edge on, we can only see a thin line extending out from both sides of the planet. At other times, we can see the rings more fully. Imagine bending down and looking at your kitchen table edge on. You can't see the top of the table, only the edge. Then stand up. Now you can see the whole top, and how long and wide the table really is.

You need

- softball
- adhesive tape
- crayons or markers
- stiff paper or poster board
- modeling clay
- a large room
- basketball
- ball of string
- small cardboard box
- paper-towel tube
- magnetic compass
- 5 chairs
- clock
- a friend
- dominos or markers
- protractor

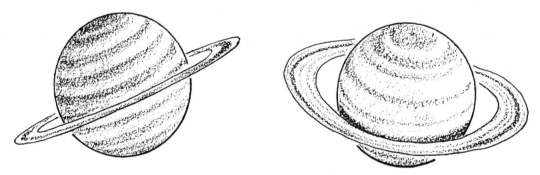

Two views of Saturn's rings

To demonstrate what can see of Saturn and its rings from Earth, try this project.

Use a softball, or similar-size ball, to represent Saturn. From stiff paper or poster board, cut a wide ring to fit around the ball. Color the ring, making bright, different colored circles going around it. Add some small dots to represent larger orbiting rocks. Tape the ring into position on the softball. Use modeling clay to form a base to hold your "softball Saturn." Using a protractor, tilt Saturn at the correct 28-degree angle for the planet.

Outside or in a large open room, place a basketball, to represent the sun, in the center. Taking some string about 31½ feet long (10½ m) and another 63 feet long (21 m), tie the ends together to make two string circles. Spread the two string circles out around the basketball. The larger circle, about 20 feet (6 m) in diameter, represents Saturn's orbit around the sun. The smaller inner circle, about 10 feet (3 m) in diameter, represents the Earth's orbit around the sun.

Now, replace the basketball, for the moment, with a clock lying on its back and facing up. Using dominos, or other such items, mark off twelve spots along the string of Saturn's orbit. To position the markers, attach a length of string to the center of the cloth and use the numbered hours as your guide. Pass a length of string straight across the face of the clock. If a friend is available to help, you each can mark off six positions by passing the string directly across the center of the cloth.

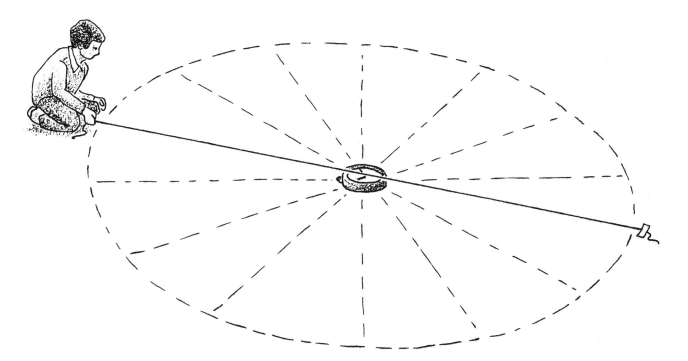

Along the inner string, representing Earth's orbit, place four chairs: one at the 12 o'clock, 3 o'clock, 6 o'clock and 9 o'clock positions. This represents the four positions, or seasons, of Earth's year.

Place a chair at the 12 o'clock position on Saturn's orbit. Put a small cardboard box on the chair and place your Saturn on it. Sit in the chair at the 12 o'clock position on Earth's orbit and look at Saturn. It should be at eye level. If it is too high, use a smaller cardboard box.

Using adhesive tape, mount a magnetic compass to the top of the cardboard box under the "softball Saturn." Where the needle points to North, draw a line on the box with a crayon or marker. During the experiment, you will be moving the Saturn chair around the room in a circle. Each time you move the chair, be sure the the compass needle lines up with the mark on the box.

With Saturn at the 12 o'clock position, sit in each of the four chairs on Earth's orbit. Pretend the empty paper-towel tube is a telescope and look through it. This is how Saturn will look from Earth for 2½ years.

Now move Saturn to the 1 o'clock position, and again sit in each of the four chairs on Earth's orbit. Each of the 12 locations for Saturn represents about 2½ years of the planet's position. Continue to do this for all 12 Saturn positions and you will see how Saturn will look from Earth for thirty years, when the cycle begins again. Did you notice the differences in the ring positions at the different times?

Project 36

Big Eye in the Sky

Tasks for a special telescope

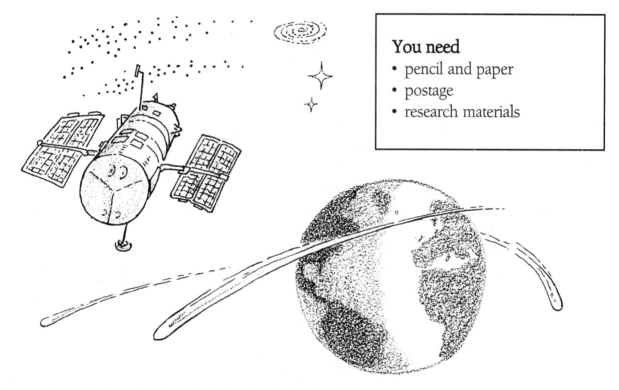

You need
- pencil and paper
- postage
- research materials

In 1990, the Space Shuttle launched the Hubble Space Telescope. This telescope orbits the Earth and provides astronomers with a new tool to use in their work. Named after Edwin Hubble, a famous American astronomer, the Hubble Space Telescope can see things too faint to be detected with telescopes on Earth. Also, because the telescope is above Earth's atmosphere, it has a much clearer view of what it sees. Objects are not distorted by the shifting gases, moisture and particles that make up the Earth's atmosphere. What does this mean? Many stars twinkle when we view them from Earth. Do they twinkle when seen by the Hubble?

Scientists propose ideas to the National Aeronautics and Space Administration (NASA) for using the Hubble Space Telescope. Your challenge is to read all you can about this great research tool and learn what it is capable of doing. Then design a job for the Hubble to do.

Write to NASA and suggest your experiment to them. What is their response?

Project 37
South of the Border
Different skies for North and South

The equator is an imaginary line around the middle of the Earth. It is located midway between the North and South Poles. The equator divides the Earth into two parts called hemispheres, or *half* spheres. Because the Earth is tilted on its axis, the Northern Hemisphere experiences summer when the Southern Hemisphere is having

> **You need**
> • pencil and paper
> • postage
> • research materials

winter. Also, those living in each hemisphere see a different part of the sky. The most famous star pattern seen in the Southern Hemisphere is the Southern Cross. One of the most famous patterns in the Northern Hemisphere is the Big Dipper.

Maps and globes often have grid lines drawn on them, called lines of latitude and longitude. These imaginary lines are used to find the location of any place on Earth.

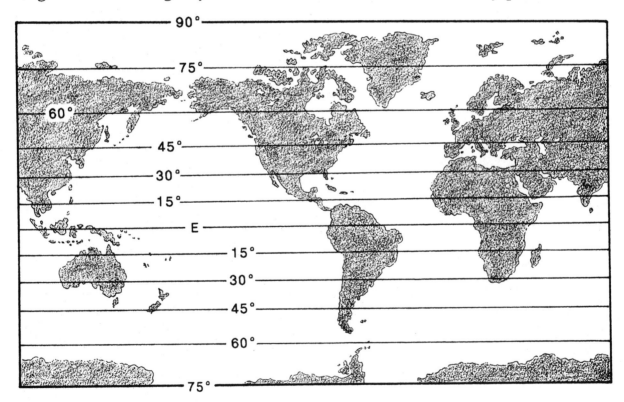

The lines measure degrees on the Earth's surface. There are 89 equally spaced lines of latitude in the Northern Hemisphere, between the equator (0 degrees) and the North Pole (90 degrees north), and 89 more in the Southern Hemisphere, between the equator (0 degrees) and the South Pole (90 degrees south).

Using an atlas or other reference book, find out the latitude where you live.
Find another city or town that lies on the same latitude as your town, but in the opposite hemisphere. If you are at 77 degrees *north*, look for a town at 77 degrees *south*. Write a letter to the board of education in the town you have selected, and tell them you would like a pen pal to write to in their school to discuss astronomy. Try to select a place where they speak the same language as you do, unless you would like a pen pal to help you learn another language or to practice a second language on.

Once you have a pen pal, share with your pal what you each see in your evening sky. Draw and exchange the popular star patterns seen in the sky, giving the names of the bigger stars and other interesting information.

Project 38

Is It Night Yet?

How long is twilight?

After the sun sets, it continues to light the Earth's atmosphere for some time. This time, between daylight and dark, is called the twilight hour, or dusk. How long does it take, after sunset, to really get dark?

On a clear evening when there's no moon in the sky, find a place nearby that is away from street or house lights. If you are in your yard, turn off any lights around your house that would keep your area from being really dark.

Find out from your daily newspaper or an almanac what time sunset will be that

evening. Just before that time, try reading a paragraph from a book and from a newspaper. Add some numbers on a solar calculator.

After the sun has set, try reading another paragraph in your book and one from the newspaper. Add some more numbers on the calculator. Do these things again every ten minutes.

How long after sunset does the solar calculator stop working? How long until you can no longer read from the book, from the newspaper? (Newspaper type is often smaller and harder to read than type in a book.)

Think of some other ways that you can measure how dark it is at a given time after sunset.

Project 39

Seeing Red, Blue, and...

Determining colors in dimming light

As the sun goes down and darkness comes, it becomes harder to see. Is it more difficult to see colors after the sun sets? If so, which colors are the hardest to identify when the light gets dim?

Draw two crossed lines on a paper plate, dividing it into four equal parts. With a red crayon or marker, color two opposite sections of the plate, and leave the other two parts white. Do the same with four other plates, using a different color—blue, orange, yellow or green—on two of the sections.

Attach a handle to each plate. You can use a ruler, tongue depressor (available at any pharmacy) or some other long and narrow wooden strip or stick. Tape your strips to the plates, leaving enough "handle" to make it easy for someone to hold the plates up.

When the sun is setting, find a safe area nearby away from bright lights. Have a friend take ten paces from you, then hold up one plate at a time, asking you the color on each plate. Then have your friend take ten more steps away from you and quiz you on the colors again. Your friend should mix up the colored plates, so they are not in the same order each time. Again, have your friend take another ten steps away from you, for a distance of 30 paces away. Can you correctly guess all the colors?

Have your friend quiz you on the colors while standing at 10 paces, 20 paces and 30 paces every ten minutes. Do this for one hour. What colors are the hardest to see? How long after sunset are you able to recognize each color?

Project 40

Color Me Warm

The effect of sunlight on colored objects

In a town in our area, the city officials thought it would be a good idea to build an ice-skating rink for the community. They formed a big rink out of asphalt and filled it with water. It got cold that winter, well below the freezing point many times. But the kids were disappointed because the water in the ice skating rink never froze! Why? It has to do with the color of asphalt—black.

The sun warms our planet. Things that are dark in color hold sunlight, and the sun's energy warms them. Things that are light in color reflect more sunlight, so are not warmed as much. What colors hold the heat from sunlight the best?

You need
- 4 empty 2-liter plastic bottles
- a 2-liter bottle of cola
- 5 thermometers
- string
- 5 sticks
- table
- sunny window
- red, blue and yellow food coloring
- pencil and paper
- clock

68

Fill four 2-liter plastic soda bottles with water. In one, add red food coloring. In another, add blue food coloring. Add yellow to another. Be sure the colors are strong and deep. Leave one bottle with just clear water. To test the color black, use a 2-liter bottle of cola soda.

Place all five bottles in a sunny window. Leave them there for about an hour.

In the meantime, cut some strings about 5 inches (13 cm) long Tie one end of each string onto each thermometer and the other end to a small stick or piece of wood. The string should be long enough so that, when the thermometer is lowered into the bottle and the stick rests on top, the bulb of the thermometer will be about halfway down the bottle.

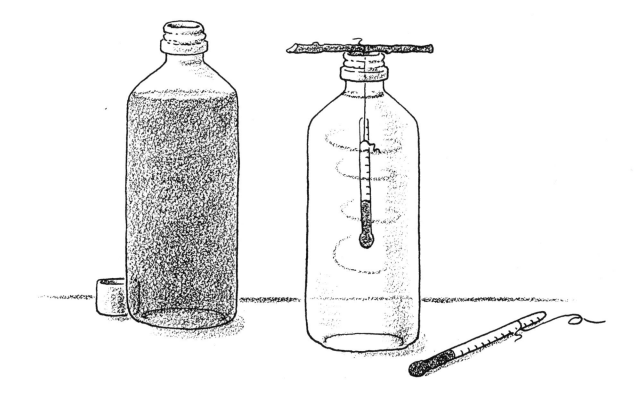

After the hour has passed, check that the thermometers all read about the same temperature. If one or two are reading higher than the others, shake them to get the temperature down. Then lower all five thermometers in the bottles, one in each, and wait five minutes. One by one, bring the thermometer up, read the temperature, write it down, and lower it again. Do this twice. If the temperature is the same, write the temperature down. If not, wait a moment and check the thermometer again, until you get the same reading a second time.

Which bottle collected the most heat energy? How can you use this information on which colors hold heat or reflect light?

Project 41

I See the Moon

Comparing views of the moon

Binoculars and telescopes have lenses that let us see distant objects up closer. On an evening when the moon is full, take a pencil and paper, look up, and draw the features and patterns you can see on the surface of the moon using only your eyes.

Then look through a pair of binoculars, opera glasses, or small telescope and draw the patterns you can see using these different optical instruments. You will be able to see more as lens strength increases. Compare the drawings. Make a list of the differences and similarities. Which instrument has the stronger or weaker lenses?

You need

- an evening with a Full Moon
- binoculars, telescope, or other viewing instrument
- pencil and paper

Project 42

Pedal Power

How high the moon?

Imagine a spaceship that runs on "pedal power," like a bicycle. Then imagine a road stretching from the Earth to the moon. If you could pedal 10 miles or kilometers per hour without stopping, how long would it take you to reach the moon? If you started now, how old would you be when you got there?

Research the distance in miles/kilometers between the Earth and the moon. Divide that by 10 per hour. The answer will be the number of hours it would take you at that speed.

Convert the number of hours for your trip into days by dividing by 24 hours, because there are 24 hours in a day. How would you convert the hours into weeks? Into years?

Once you know how long the trip would take, add that time to your age today. Exactly how old would you be when you got there if you left today? How old when you got back?

Astronomers have to work with big numbers and long periods of time like this every day, because of the vastness of space. Mathematics is a very important part of astronomy.

Project 43

Words Crossing

Creating science puzzles

Make your own crossword puzzle using words related to flight, space and astronomy. First select a topic, such as "Flight." Then think of a dozen or so words to use in the puzzle; for example, pitch, yaw, roll, plane, flight, lift, balloon, altimeter, climb, propeller, drag, plane, jet, airport. Shaping all those words into a crossword puzzle may seem hard to do, but there is a trick that can make it much easier.

You need
• pencil
• graph paper with large blocks
• scissors

Take a sheet of grid paper with large-sized squares and print the list of words across, one letter to each block. Then print the words a second time, but this time write them reading down

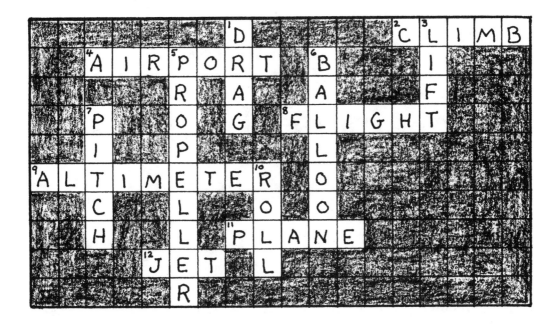

instead of across. Take a pair of scissors and cut out each word. Place the longest word (going across) on a clean sheet of grid paper. Lay other words over it, reading down, wherever the letters match. Then continue to lay more words over the other words. Once you use a word, set aside the second copy of that word, because you only want to use each word once in the puzzle. Juggle the words around until you have a nicely shaped crossword puzzle. Leave out words that just won't fit in, and add other words you think of while you're constructing the puzzle that will work okay and fit the topic.

Next, research the meaning of each word and write some clues. In the first block of each word (starting at the top, then right to left), number the word. Match your definitions to the numbers and separate the clues into Across and Down columns.

Color in the empty blocks on the paper, in and around your puzzle, where no letters appear. Lift the beginning of each word carefully, one by one, and write the word number in the blank square under the first letter before you remove the word. Write the number in the upper left-hand corner as small as you can. You need to leave room for the person working the puzzle to fill in the letter.

Make several copies of your crossword puzzle so that you can hand them out and more of your friends can enjoy it.

Science Crosswords

"Planetary Words" might include: Saturn, Mars, Jupiter, Venus, Mercury, orbit, ellipse, ring, rotate, axis.

"Astronomy" might include the words: asteroid, galaxy, comet, nebula, nova, pulsar, planetarium, telescope, astrolabe, meteor, star.

Project 44

Screened Images

How the eye sees

Binoculars and telescopes use lenses to magnify images. But the first optical tool ever used in astronomy is actually the human eye. Objects reflect light that enters the eye through the pupil, then passes through a lens that focuses the image onto the area at the back of your eye called the retina (something like film in a camera).

You need
- hand magnifying glass
- modeling clay
- a few small toys
- high-intensity desk lamp
- adhesive tape
- strip of stiff white paper
- table
- scissors
- an adult

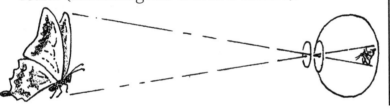

Let's set up a demonstration of how the lens works in your eye and in a telescope. Using modeling clay, form a base to hold a small, hand magnifying glass upright and place it on a table. At the other end of the table, place a few small toys (blocks, trucks, dolls) in a group. Have an adult plug in a high-intensity desk lamp and shine the bright light on the toys.

Hold a 3-inch-wide (8-cm) strip of stiff white paper next to the lens of the magnifying glass, on the side opposite the lamp and toys. Slowly move the paper away from the lens until the image of the toys appears in focus. This is the correct imaging distance. Roll the paper strip into an eye-shaped curve. Fix the paper into this correct position by taping the two ends of the paper strip to the magnifying glass lens.

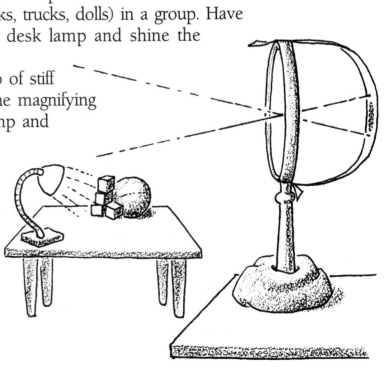

Project 45
Focus on Light Beams
Understanding the refracting telescope

A telescope is an instrument that allows distant objects to appear close up. Its name comes from the Greek words *tele*, meaning "from afar," and *skopos*, "viewer." Telescopes gather light and focus it, making objects appear nearer than they really are and letting us see them in more detail. Even the simplest telescope reveals things in the sky that the unaided eye cannot see: the rings of Saturn, craters on the moon, and the bands around Jupiter. In 1608, the Italian scientist Galileo Galilei was the first astronomer to use a telescope. There are different kinds of telescope. One that uses two lenses, instead of one, is called a refracting telescope.

Stand two magnifying glasses up by sticking their handles in bases made of clay. Set each lens on a piece of cardboard. Place one magnifying glass in the middle of a table by a window. Hold a piece of white paper next to the magnifying glass, on the side opposite the window. Slowly move the paper away from the magnifying glass until an image of objects outside the window is projected in focus on the paper. Now, take away the paper, and stand the second magnifying glass at that exact spot. Place your eye next to the second magnifying glass and slowly move away from it until an image of objects outside comes in focus. Do the objects appear bigger? You have made a simple telescope.

Project 46

Clean Sweep
Earth's changing surfaces

The surfaces of planets, asteroids and moons that do not have an atmosphere record things that take place and preserve them for thousands of years. Planets, such as the Earth, that do have atmospheres have constantly changing surfaces. On the Earth, wind, rain, heat from the sun, freezing temperatures and other atmospheric events wear away and change many features. Compare the surface of the moon to Earth's surface. The Moon is covered with giant and small craters, recording a history of meteor hits. How many of these types of craters do you know of on Earth? Meteor Crater in Arizona is one of the very few. Show that the atmosphere of the Earth changes its surface features.

You need
- fine sand
- a 3-liter plastic bottle
- scissors
- 2 small wood screws
- screwdriver
- 2 small blocks
- water
- a week
- log book
- pencil
- an adult

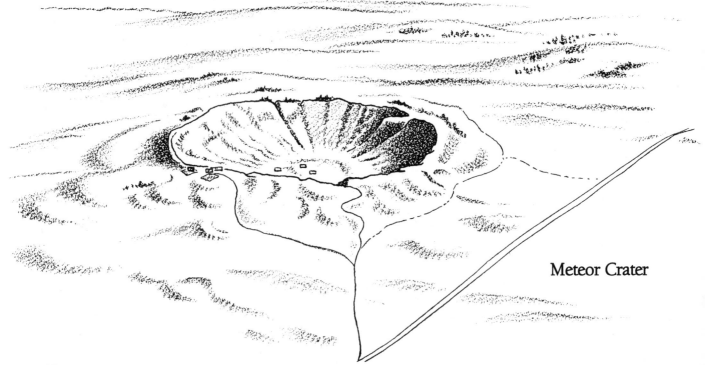

Meteor Crater

76

Ask an adult to cut a 3-liter plastic bottle in half lengthwise, that is, from top to bottom. Lay the two halves open on a table. For one of the bottles, form a mound of modeling clay and position it under the bottom section. This will give this bottle half a slight pitch so that rain will run off.

Fill both bottle halves with very fine sand. Add a small amount of water to each of the bottles of sand. Mold features in the wet sand to represent the surface of a planet; make mountains, craters, small mounds, and deep crevices.

Keep one bottle inside in a protected place, away from open windows and sunlight. Put the bottle with the raised section outside on a picnic table or bench where it will be exposed to whatever happens—rain, sunlight and wind—but will not be disturbed by other people or animals. The bottle that stays inside the house represents objects in space that do not have atmospheres, like the moon and Mercury. The outside bottle represents a planet with an active atmosphere. In a log book, write down the date the project began.

At the end of a week, compare the surfaces of the two bottles. Write down any observations you make about the features on the surfaces. In what way did the mountains, the crevices and the craters change? Were any new features added?

Project 47

On the Level

Flight terms: pitch, roll, yaw

When an airplane is flying through the air, there are three ways it can change its flight. The point around which it moves is the plane's center of gravity, an imaginary point where the plane is balanced.

An axis is the imaginary line around which something turns. Astronomers talk about the Earth rotating on its axis, the imaginary line extending through the North and South Poles. The plural of the word axis is axes.

In an airplane, three imaginary axes can be drawn through the plane's balancing point. One axis extends from in front of the plane through the body of it and out the back. When the plane turns on this axis, one wing becomes lower than the other, and the movement is called *roll*.

You need
- large cardboard box
- small toy model airplane
- string
- several pencils
- crayons, paints or construction paper
- tape
- cotton
- model houses and toy cars (optional)

Another axis extends from the top of the plane through the bottom. The plane can turn to one side or the other along this axis. This turning movement is called *yaw*.

The third axis extends from the left side of the plane through the right, parallel to

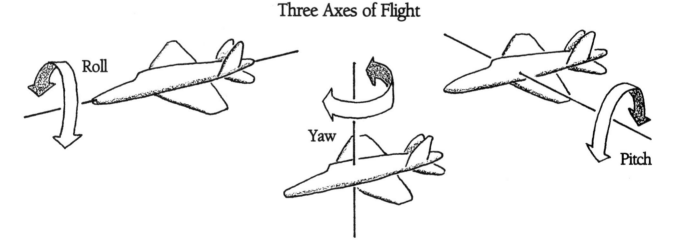

Three Axes of Flight

Roll

Yaw

Pitch

the wings. The front of the plane can move up or down around this axis. This movement is called *pitch*.

To demonstrate these three motions, build a flight scene and show how an airplane moves around these three axes.

Remove the flaps from a good-sized cardboard box and lay it on its side. Using crayons, paints or construction paper, make a sky scene inside the box with a ground scene, trees and roads, at the bottom. You may want to include small model houses and cars on the landscape and place puffs of cotton in the sky for clouds.

Tie a string to the center balancing point of a toy airplane. Hold the plane up by the string. You may need to tie another short string to the plane and attach it to the hanging string in order to make the plane balance correctly. Then poke a small hole in the top of the box, and push the end of the hanging string up through it. Tie the string to a pencil or stick to hold the plane in place.

With your hand, demonstrate the pitch, roll and yaw movements. To really show roll, put tape or a rubber band on a pencil or dowel and push against the lower end of the tail to roll the plane.

The wings and shorter tail wings of airplanes have parts called ailerons, elevators and rudders. These devices control either pitch, roll or yaw. Learn their names and the airplane movements they control.

Project 48

Big Splash
When a meteor falls

Scientists aren't sure where they come from, but meteorites have been found all over the world. Are they pieces of the moon, Mars, the asteroid belt or from deep space? Chunks of stone or iron traveling through space are called meteoroids. If they pass close enough to the Earth, the Earth's gravity can capture them and pull them into its atmosphere, then they are given another name, meteors. The meteors are soon falling so fast that friction from passing through the atmosphere heats them and they melt, providing a spectacular show called shooting stars. Usually, meteors are small and burn up completely in the atmosphere. Those that do reach the ground are called

You need
- some chicken wire
- newspaper
- liquid white glue or paste
- large, 3-inch-deep (8-cm) roasting pan
- modeling clay
- Ping-Pong ball
- golf ball
- water
- ruler

meteorites. Most meteorites are small, but some very large ones have been found and can be seen in science museums. What would happen if a large meteor crashed into a body of water, such as a lake, bay or ocean? Would it cause a wave and raise the level of the water?

The heaviness of an object depends on its mass, how dense it is (how much it is packed together). A Ping-Pong ball is about the same size as a golf ball, but a golf ball is much denser, so has more mass. With size equal, which would cause a higher wave, a meteorite with less mass or one with more mass?

Form a hypothesis that, if two meteorites were about the same size and moving at about the same rate of speed, the one having the more mass would create a bigger wave. Prove it.

In a large-size roasting pan, about 1 by 2 feet (30 by 60 cm), pack a layer of modeling clay at one end. Build the layer up until it forms a flat mound 2 inches (5 cm) high and about 4 inches (10 cm) wide, extending from one side of the pan to the other. Use some chicken wire, or other support structure, to form a mountain about 4 to 5 inches (10 to 13 cm) high. Tear thin strips of newspaper and coat

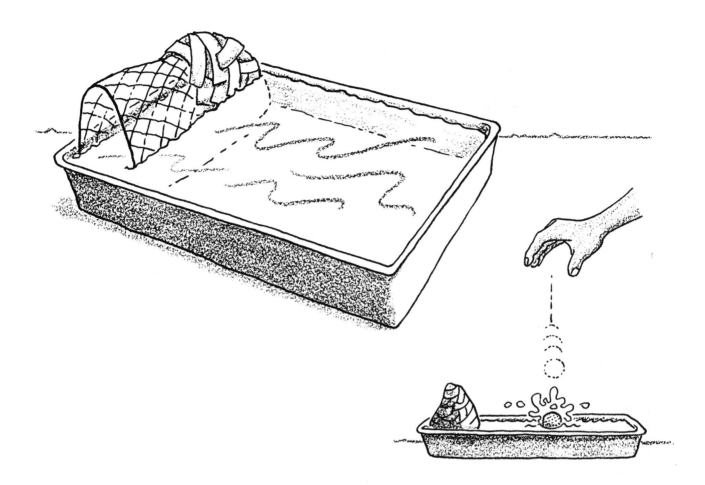

them with liquid white glue or paste. Using a crisscross pattern, cover the whole mountain frame. Let it dry a few days, then put another layer on it. You may want to paint it to look like a mountain.

Set the mountain on the layer of clay in the roasting pan. Place the pan in a bathtub or someplace outside where spilled water won't cause a problem. Fill the pan with water until it is level with the top of the modeling clay.

From a height of 2 feet (60 cm) above the pan, drop a Ping-Pong ball into the water. Inspect your mountain for the wet mark that shows how far the wave from the impact of the ball traveled up its side. Using a ruler, measure the height from the base of the mountain, at water level, to the water mark on the mountain. Write down the distance from the water level, at rest, to the water mark. Let the mountainside dry.

When the side of the mountain has dried, drop a golf ball from the same height as the you dropped the earlier ball, 2 feet (60 cm) above the pan. Again, measure the height of the water mark on the side of the mountain.

Although both balls have about the same size and shape, one has more mass than the other. Which ball caused the larger wave? What would happen if you dropped the same size ball of clay?

Project 49

Mirror, Mirror

Comparing heat from direct and reflected sunlight

Have you ever stood by a window and felt the warmth from the sun coming in? In the winter, a sunny window feels really good! Is sunlight reflected by a mirror as warm as direct sunlight?

Lay two thermometers side by side in a shaded place in a room. After five minutes, read the temperatures on each thermometer. They should be the same. If one reads higher than the other, mark the thermometer so you'll know which one it is. Write down how many degrees higher that thermometer is reading. To compare the two temperatures at the end of the project, this number will have to be subtracted from the reading on the higher thermometer.

Place a table by a sunny window. Put a second table in another part of the room where there is no direct sunlight. Take two small pieces of modeling clay and stick a thermometer in each one *upside down*, with the bulb end of the thermometers sticking up into the air.

You need
- 2 thermometers
- a mirror
- modeling clay
- a sunny window
- 2 tables
- an adult

Place one thermometer in direct sunlight on the table by the sunny window. Place the other thermometer on the table away from any sunlight. Place a mirror on the table by the sunny window and reflect the sunlight onto the second thermometer. Hold it there for five minutes.

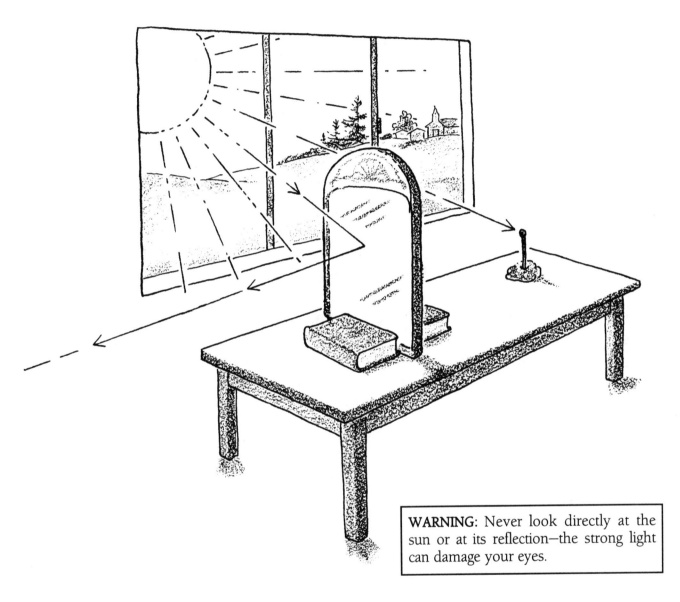

WARNING: Never look directly at the sun or at its reflection—the strong light can damage your eyes.

Now read the temperature on each thermometer. Remember, if both of the thermometers did not read the same temperature before they were placed in the sunlight, the one that read higher will now need that original difference in degrees subtracted from its current reading.

Compare the two temperatures. Where they both the same or was one warmer than the other? If so, which one was warmer?

Project 50

Darth Fader

Effect of sunlight on color

The sun's light makes life on Earth possible, but it can also be damaging. Too much sunlight can give us a bad sunburn. It causes colors in rugs and upholstered chairs and couches to fade.

Cut three columns out of a newspaper. Cut three strips from a sheet of red construction paper, three from a sheet of green construction paper, and three from a sheet of blue construction paper.

On a large piece of cardboard, tape up one of the newspaper columns, and the strips of red, green and blue construction paper. Do the same on another large piece of cardboard.

You need
- a newspaper
- sheet of red construction paper
- sheet of green construction paper
- sheet of blue construction paper
- a sunny window
- 2 tables
- adhesive tape
- scissors
- large piece of cardboard
- 3 envelopes

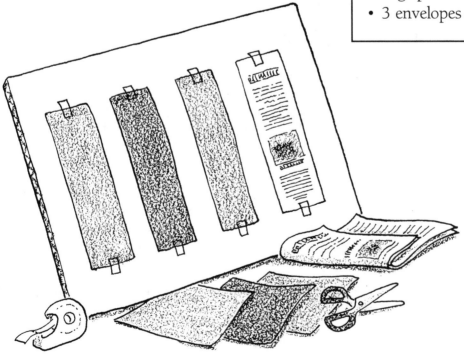

Place the last newspaper column and three colored paper strips in an envelope, and put it away in a dresser drawer, out of the light.

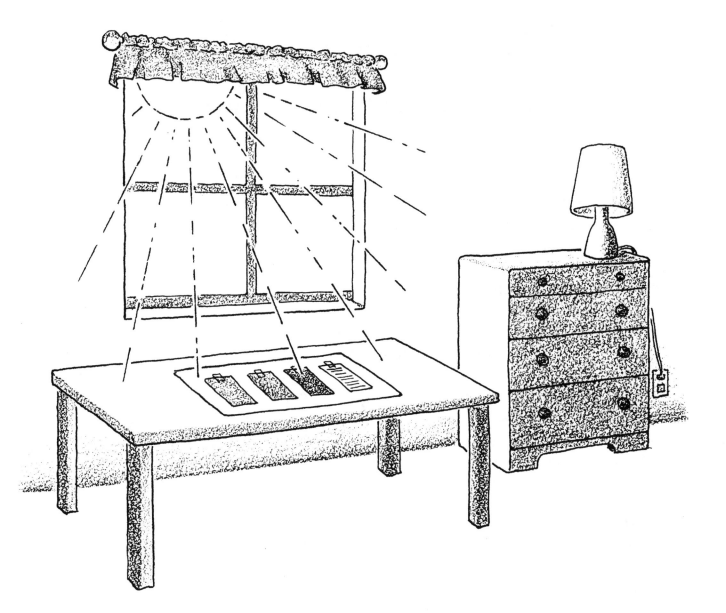

During a day when the sun is shining in the windows, lay one of the cardboard sheets on the table in direct sunlight. Stand the other cardboard sheet on a table in the room that does not get sunlight, only light that is normally in the room (reflected sunlight and light from room lamps).

Continue the experiment on sunny days for several weeks, recording the amount of time the taped-up strips are exposed to the sun and the light. Then compare all of the strips, including the ones that have been stored in the envelopes.

Which ones faded the most?

Project 51

The Eyes Have It

Light's effect on night viewing

The eye is an amazing optical instrument. Our eyes are sensitive enough to be able to see such dim objects as faint stars, but can adjust to allow us to see well in bright light. The reason is that the pupil, an opening in the eye that lets light enter, gets larger and smaller. The iris, the colored area surrounding the pupil (brown eyes, blue eyes), expands and contracts to adjust the pupil's opening to smaller in bright light and larger in dim light.

You need
- a metal coat hanger
- flash camera, or bright spotlight or flashlight
- dark, cloudless night
- a friend
- pencil and paper

When it detects bright light, the iris responds instantly to protect the eyes from the brightness. But it takes about ten minutes for the iris to contract in dim light in order to fully open the pupil. That is why, when using the naked eye to study the night sky, we need to give our eyes time to adjust to the darkness before we can see faint stars.

To get an idea of just how many more faint stars the eye can see when it is fully adjusted to darkness, go outside on a dark, cloudless night and wait about ten minutes for your eyes to adjust. Take a metal coat hanger and bend the triangle to make a square. Turn it upside down and use the hanger's hook as a handle.

Find something to use as a reference point—the top of a tree or flagpole, or a fence post or chimney—when looking through your viewer frame at an area of the sky. Hold the viewer at arm's length and look through it, aligning the bottom corner with your reference point. Count the number of stars you can see in that part of the sky. Write down your observation.

Now have a friend stand about 5 or 6 feet (2 m) in front of you and pretend to take your picture with a flash camera. (No film is needed, just the bright light of the flash hitting your eyes.) Again, hold the hanger at arm's length and align it to your reference point. How many stars do you count now?

How long does it take before the pupils of your eyes have adjusted to the darkness once again, and you can see all the faint stars that you did at first?

Does the distance your friend stands from you affect the number of stars you can see after the flash? Try having your friend stand 9 feet (3 m) away, 20 feet (8 m) away, and then 30 feet (12 m), counting the stars between each flash distance to test the effect on your eyes. How far away does your friend have to stand before the flash doesn't affect your ability to see faint stars?

Project 52

It Came from Space

What we've learned from space research

The exploration of space has not only increased our knowledge about our world and the universe we live in, it has also benefited people in many other ways. Can you think of things we have and can do because of our struggles to go to the moon

You need
- research materials
- pencil and paper

and send unmanned spacecraft to Mars and outside our solar system? Go to the library and research some of the ways that we have benefited from "spin-offs" of the space industry. Look into advances in communication and medicine, the miniaturization of electronics, and the development of materials used to make modern products.

What life-science knowledge has been learned by experiments carried into space? Is it possible to grow plants in a space garden, without earth and with artificial sunlight? The space shuttle, for example, once carried a spider aloft to see if it would spin a web in the weightlessness of space. What happened?

What experiments can you think of that could be proposed for a future space shuttle mission?

Project 53

Time after Time

Timeline space: highlights of the age of space exploration

A timeline, listing what happened when, allows us to make connections and easily see how knowledge has advanced and history has been made. Create a timeline showing the major events in man's exploration of space with manned and unmanned spacecraft.

Another timeline might show the major events in astronomy that led up to the space age of the mid-1900s. You could start with the invention of the telescope, and include events leading up to the launch of the first successful liquid-propellant rocket by Robert Goddard in 1926. Names to research: Newton, Herschel, Galileo, Kepler.

You need
- pencil and paper
- research materials
- art supplies

Hubble 1993
Venus probes 1981
Pioneer 1978
Mars photos 1975
Neil Armstrong
1st Woman in Space
Y. Gargarin
Explorer-1
Robert Goddard
Newton
Kepler
Galileo

Galileo
Newton
Kepler

WORDS TO KNOW

A science glossary

asteroid A small planetoid or chunk of rock revolving around the sun; most travel between the orbits of Mars and Jupiter. Asteroids that stray in our direction may become meteors.

axis A straight line on which an object turns. The imaginary line from the North to the South Pole is the Earth's axis. Plural is *axes*.

center of gravity The point at which the total weight of an object balances.

centrifugal force A force that pushes outward when an object is moving in a curve.

comet A packed collection of gas, dust and ice crystals that move around the sun in orbits that take them outside the solar system.

constellation An observed pattern of stars, used to help locate and identify individual stars and other celestial bodies, such as the Northern Hemisphere's constellation Orion.

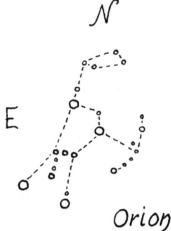

drag An aviation term for the resistance of air to the forward motion of an aircraft. The drag force tries to slow the plane down the faster it moves through the air.

eclipse When one body blocks out the light from a more distant body.

equator An imaginary circle that is midway between the north and south poles of a sphere.

equinox A time of the year during the Earth's movement around the sun when the North and South Poles are equally distant from the sun. The vernal equinox occurs in the spring. The autumnal equinox occurs in the fall.

gravity A force of attraction between two objects.

Hubble Space Telescope A sensitive telescope orbiting the Earth. It lets astronomers study the stars without having to look through the Earth's atmosphere, which can make it hard to see and cause distortion.

hypothesis   A thoughtful, reasoned guess about something, based on what is known. A hypothesis must be proven by experimentation.

latitude/longitude   Angular distances on a globe: parallel, or lateral, to the equator is called latitude; lengthwise, from a designated zero-degree meridian, is longitude.

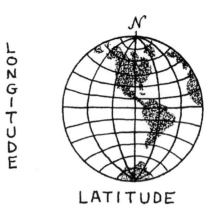

light pollution   The brightness of light other than the light from the stars, which spoils your view of the night sky.

light-year   Not a measure of time; a light-year measures the distance light travels through space in a year, about 5.9 trillion miles (9.5 trillion kilometers). Not counting our own sun, a star that is only eight light-minutes away, it takes the light from Proxima Centauri, our closest star, 4.2 light-years to reach us.

magnetism   A force recognized by the ability of certain objects to attract iron.

magnitude   A standard measurement of the brightness of stars.

mass   The density of "stuff" packed into an object. The more mass something has, the heavier it is. A Ping-Pong ball and a golf ball are about the same size and shape, but a golf ball has more mass.

meteor, meteoroid, meteorite   Chunks of debris traveling through space are called meteoroids. When a meteoroid enters the Earth's atmosphere it is called a meteor. Most meteors burn up completely from friction in the Earth's atmosphere, but when one hits the ground it is called a meteorite. Meteor Crater in Arizona is believed to be the impact site of a long-ago meteor strike.

observation   Using your senses—smelling, touching, looking, listening and tasting—to study something closely, sometimes over a long period of time.

orbit   The path an object takes around another celestial body.

pitch   One of the three axes of flight. The movement of a plane around an imaginary line, or axis, extending from the left side of the plan and out through the right (parallel to the wings) is called pitch. The front and the back of the plane tilts up or down.

plane of the solar system   An imaginary line through the Earth's orbit that extends out past the planets. Think of the sun being in the middle and all the planets resting on a vast flat surface. (Pluto is the only planet that is a little above the plane of the solar system).

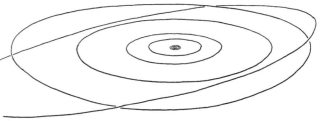

planet   A massive body that orbits a sun and shines by reflecting its light. Our solar system has nine major planets and many minor planets, or asteroids.

roll   One of the three axes of flight. An imaginary line can be drawn from the front of the plane out through the back (an axis). When the plane tilts on this axis, one wing becomes lower than the other. The tilting movement along this axis is called roll.

star   A very hot, glowing ball of gases. The sun is our closest star.

telescope   From the Greek words *tele*, "from afar," and *skopos*, "viewer." An instrument that collects light and, with lenses, enables us to see faraway objects up close and with more detail. The Italian scientist Galileo Galilei, in 1608, was the first astronomer to use a telescope.

trajectory   The path of an object as it travels through the air.

twilight   The part of the evening after the sun sets, when the Earth's atmosphere continues to reflect the sun's light. Twilight lasts for about an hour after the sun goes down.

waning/waxing   Observed changes of the moon's phases. When the phase of the moon is between being completely dark (New Moon) and completely illuminated (Full Moon), it is said to be waxing, or building its way up to a Full Moon. When the phase of the moon is between a Full Moon and a New Moon, it is said to be waning, showing less and less light until it isn't lit at all. Then the cycle repeats.

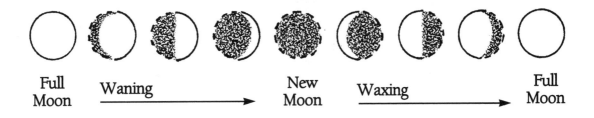

yaw   One of the three axes of flight. An imaginary line (axis) can be drawn from the top of the plane out through the bottom. The plane can turn to one side or the other along this axis. This turning movement is called yaw.

Index

About the Authors

BOB BONNET, who holds a master's degree in environmental education, has been teaching science at the junior high school level for over 25 years. He was a state naturalist at Belleplain State Forest in New Jersey. Mr. Bonnet has organized and judged many science fairs at both the local and regional levels. He has served as the chairman of the science curriculum committee for the Dennis Township school system and is a science teaching fellow at Rowan College in New Jersey.

DAN KEEN holds an Associate in Science degree, having majored in electronic technology. He is the owner and publisher of a newspaper in New Jersey. He was employed in the field of electronics for 23 years, and his work included computer consulting and programming. Mr. Keen has written numerous articles for many computer magazines and trade journals since 1979. He is the co-author of several computer programming books. For ten years, he taught computer courses for adults in four schools. In 1986 and 1987, he taught computer science at Stockton State College in New Jersey.

Together, Mr. Bonnet and Mr. Keen have had many articles and books published on a variety of science topics. They are the co-authors of two other books, *Science Fair Projects: Environmental Science* and *Science Fair Projects: Electricity and Electronics*, also published by Sterling Publishing Company.